# Lecture Notes in Computer Science　　　10561

Commenced Publication in 1973
Founding and Former Series Editors:
Gerhard Goos, Juris Hartmanis, and Jan van Leeuwen

More information about this series at http://www.springer.com/series/7407

Yong Dou · Haixiang Lin
Guangyu Sun · Junjie Wu
Dora Heras · Luc Bougé (Eds.)

# Advanced Parallel Processing Technologies

12th International Symposium, APPT 2017
Santiago de Compostela, Spain, August 29, 2017
Proceedings

Springer

*Editors*
Yong Dou
National University of Defense Technology
Changsha
China

Junjie Wu
National University of Defense Technology
Changsha
China

Haixiang Lin
Delft University of Technology
Delft
The Netherlands

Dora Heras
CiTIUS
Santiago de Compostela
Spain

Guangyu Sun
Peking University
Beijing
China

Luc Bougé
ENS Rennes
Rennes
France

ISSN 0302-9743             ISSN 1611-3349   (electronic)
Lecture Notes in Computer Science
ISBN 978-3-319-67951-8       ISBN 978-3-319-67952-5   (eBook)
DOI 10.1007/978-3-319-67952-5

Library of Congress Control Number: 2017953429

LNCS Sublibrary: SL1 – Theoretical Computer Science and General Issues

Printed on acid-free paper

This Springer imprint is published by Springer Nature
The registered company is Springer International Publishing AG
The registered company address is: Gewerbestrasse 11, 6330 Cham, Switzerland

# Preface

The ever-increasing demand of parallel processing drives society to investigate new computer architecture and system software techniques. Following this trend, APPT 2017 broadly captured the recent advances in big data processing, parallel architectures and systems, parallel software, parallel algorithms and artificial intelligence applications, distributed and cloud computing, etc., and provided an excellent forum for the presentation of research efforts and the exchange of viewpoints.

We would like to express our gratitude to all the colleagues who submitted papers and congratulate those whose papers were accepted. Following the success of its past ten conference series, APPT 2017 managed to provide a high-quality program for all attendees. The Program Committee (PC) decided to accept 11 papers. All submissions were reviewed by three PC members. There was also an online discussion stage to guarantee that consensus was reached for each submission.

While we would like to thank the authors for submitting their nice work to APPT 2017, and we would also like to show our sincere appreciation to PC members. The 25 PC members did an excellent job in returning high-quality reviews in time and engaging in a constructive online discussion. We would also like to thank the general chairs (Prof. Yong Dou and Prof. Haixiang Lin), the publicity chair (Prof. Duo Liu), and the publication chair (Siqi Shen). Our thanks also go to Springer for its assistance in putting the proceedings together. Finally, we offer our special thanks to the Organizing Committees of EuroPar, who made it possible to co-locate APPT 2017 with EuroPar 2017 in Spain.

July 2017

Guangyu Sun
Yiran Chen

# Organization

APPT 2017 was organized by the China Computer Federation.

## General Chairs

Yong Dou            National University of Defense Technology, China
Hai Xiang Lin       Delft University of Technology, The Netherlands

## Steering Committee

Zhenzhou Ji         Harbin Institute of Technology, China
Dongsheng Wang    Tsinghua University, China
Xingwei Wang       Northeastern University, China
Minyou Wu          Shanghai Jiaotong University, China
Gongxuan Zhang    Nanjing University of Science and Technology, China
Junjie Wu           National University of Defense Technology, China

## Publication Chair

Siqi Shen           National University of Defense Technology, China

## Publicity Chair

Duo Liu             Chongqing University, China

## Program Chairs

Guangyu Sun       Peking University, China
Yiran Chen          Duke University, USA

## Program Committee

Aske Plaat          Leiden University, The Netherlands
Chao Li             Shanghai Jiao Tong University, China
Chun Jason Xue     City University of Hong Kong, Hong Kong, SAR China
Cong Xu            HP Labs, USA
Dongsheng Li       National University of Defense Technology, China
Eric Postma        Tilburg University, The Netherlands
Felix Xiaozhu Lin    Purdue University, USA
Guihai Yan         ICT, Chinese Academy of Sciences, China
Huiyang Zhou       North Carolina State University, USA

# Contents

# Platform-Adaptive High-Throughput Surveillance Video Condensation on Heterogeneous Processor Clusters

Peng Qiao[1(✉)], Teng Li[1], Yong Dou[1], Yuanwu Lei[1], Hongbing Luo[2], and Chi Jin[3]

[1] National Laboratory for Parallel and Distributed Processing, School of Computer, National University of Defense Technology, Changsha 410073, China
{pengqiao,liteng09,yongdou,yuanwulei}@nudt.edu.cn
[2] Institute of Applied Physics and Computational Mathematics, Beijing, China
hbluo@iapcm.ac.cn
[3] School of Computer Science and Technology, University of South China, Hengyang, China
jinchi997@aliyun.com

**Abstract.** Directly browsing and analyzing numerous surveillance videos is inefficient for human operators. Video condensation is a technical solution to fast video browsing. On the one hand, traditional video condensation methods that skip frames using simple strategies may lose some important frames. On the other hand, the methods that rearrange frame contexts improve the browsing efficiency, but are not easy to be accelerated using the data processing centers with various hardware configurations. In this paper, we propose a platform-adaptive video condensation system based on change detection, which is easy to accelerate and keeps important frames accurately. To take full advantage of hardware acceleration, we implement each module of the proposed system using multithreading and GPU acceleration, and then further accelerate the system by exploiting the task-level parallelism. We solve the computational resources assignment problem via local search method. To be platform-adaptive, the combination of module using different hardware acceleration are compared to choose the optimal combination to make full use of the computational resources. Detailed experiments are conducted to validate the accuracy of the proposed system, the efficiency of the platform-adaptive mechanism and the high throughput performance.

**Keywords:** Change detection · Multithreading acceleration · GPU acceleration · CPU-GPU heterogeneous acceleration · Task-level parallelism · Video condensation

## 1 Introduction

In the past decades, numerous surveillance cameras have been deployed in public areas in China. In particular, over 20,000 security cameras have been installed in the prefecture-level cities. Approximately 80% of these cameras are @720P, whereas the

Y. Dou et al. (Eds.): APPT 2017, LNCS 10561, pp. 1–13, 2017.
DOI: 10.1007/978-3-319-67952-5_1

remaining 20% are @1080P. According to related regulations, the data recorded by these cameras should be stored for at least 30 days. The amount of video data can reach over 15,000 terabytes. Due to the high cost and reliability issues, it is impractical for human operators to continuously monitor the huge amount of video data. Therefore, the efficient browsing of long surveillance videos is becoming increasingly crucial in the public security field.

Several approaches for browsing videos have been proposed in literature. These methods can be roughly grouped into two categories. The methods in the first group condense the original video in the temporal domain. In methods [1, 2], videos can be quickly browsed by skipping several frames to reach the selected timestamp or between selected frames. Consequently, certain data may be overlooked if the skipped frames contain important information. To keep more important frames, the adaptive methods of skipping frames [3, 4] are proposed. These adaptive methods skip frames in periods of low activity, and keep frames in periods of high activity.

The methods in the second group condense the original video in spatial and temporal domain. In [5], the space-time video montage is used to analyze the spatial and temporal information distributions of the original video. However, the visual quality of the condensed video is unsatisfactory, because it has obvious seams and some pieces of information are lost. In [6], a ribbon carving-based method is proposed. This technique considers a ribbon, a flexible frame without activity, as the smallest processing unit and iteratively removes all of them from the original video until no ribbon is left. However, it may fail to handle scenarios where adjacent objects move in different speeds and directions. The obtained condensed video also has obvious seams. Video synopsis [7–9] methods consider a tube, a frame sequence of an object, as the smallest unit and merge tubes by solving an optimization problem. While they provide superior performance, the tube-based methods are low computational efficiency compared with the previous methods. A high-performance condensation system for online videos was proposed in [10]. This system achieves high throughput performance by using a graphics processor unit (GPU) and a multi-core acceleration.

## 1.1 Motivations and Contributions

Though temporal-spatial methods provide high condensation ratio, these methods cannot provide high computational efficiency. On the contrary, temporal condensation methods are time efficient but may loss important frames. To this end, we employ change detection to achieve temporal condensation, which only remove the frames that contains minimal or no activities. The contributions of this paper are summarized as follow.

**Promising Performance in Keeping Important Frames.** The proposed system exploit change detection with object detection to keep important frames, which keeps more important frames compared with simple temporal skimming or forwarding and provides competing performance compared with the temporal-spatial condensation methods.

**Efficient Platform Adaptation.** To make full use of the computational resources in the platform with different hardware configurations, we combine the modules of the proposed system and exploit a local search to efficiently optimize the computational resources assignment for each combination.

**High Throughput Performance.** Each module of the proposed video condensation system was implemented using both multithreading and GPU acceleration, and further accelerated using task-level parallelism. On platform with 2-cores CPU @ 3.20 GHz and GTX550Ti (described in Table 2), the proposed system condensed one-hour videos @352 × 288 in about 60 s, and achieved 2.6 MB/s throughput and 1426.3 frames per second (fps) performances.

## 2  Change Detection Based Video Condensation Framework

The proposed change detection based video condensation (CDVC) framework is illustrated in Fig. 1. This framework can be divided into three modules, namely module FRM, MT, and OBJWRT. In module FRM, the images are captured and buffered. In module MT, change detection procedure is conducted based on background subtraction. In module OBJWRT, the objects are determined via connected component labelling and the frames with objects are written to the output video.

**Original**           **Condensed**
video               video

**Fig. 1.**  CDVC framework in module view.

### 2.1  Background Building and Updating

Change detection techniques can be categorized into two groups, namely background subtraction [14–21] and frame difference [22, 23]. Frame difference is fast, but fails to detect objects when they stop or move slowly. By contrast, background subtraction may not encounter such problem. To achieve both high detection accuracy and computational efficiency, we adopt the simplest parameter estimation method to build and update the background image.

In parameter estimation-based background subtraction, the background image $I_{bg}$ is the mean of the buffered images $B = \{I_i\}_{i=1}^{N_{bg}}$ as,

$$I_{bg} = \frac{1}{N_{bg}} \sum_{i=1}^{N_{bg}} I_i, \tag{1}$$

where $N_{bg}$ is the number of images in $B$. To estimate $I_{bg}$ accurately, $N_{bg}$ is usually large. It is memory-consuming to buffer all images $\{I_i\}_{i=1}^{N_{bg}}$. To be memory-efficient, we buffer

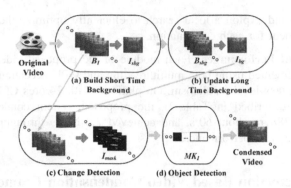

**Fig. 2.** Flowchart of CDVC framework.

$N_{sbg}$ short time background images $B_s = \{I_{sbg}\}_{i=1}^{N_{sbg}}$, as shown in Fig. 2(a) and (b). Therefore, Eq. (1) can be reformulated as,

$$I_{bg} = \frac{1}{N_{sbg}} \sum_{i=1}^{N_{sbg}} \left( \frac{N_{sbg}}{N_{bg}} \sum_{I \in B_l^i} I \right) = \frac{1}{N_{sbg}} \sum_{i=1}^{N_{sbg}} I_{sbg}^i \tag{2}$$

### 2.2   Change Detection

When $I_{bg}$ is updated or built, the activities are determined by comparing the $I_{bg}$ and the new buffered image $I_i$, as shown in Fig. 2(c), and formulated as,

$$I_{mask}^i = \begin{cases} 1, & if \; |I_i - I_{bg}| > Th \\ 0, & otherwise \end{cases}, \tag{3}$$

where $Th$ is an empirical parameter. The value 1 and 0 in Eq. (3) imply that the corresponding pixel probably belongs to a moving object and to a non-moving object (or the background), respectively.

### 2.3   Object Detection

Candidate objects are considered as connected components [24, 25], which are found within $I_{mask}$. These candidate objects ($Cont$) are considered as objects when satisfying some geometric constrains, such as the area of candidate objects ($A_{cont}$), formulating as

$$MK_l^i = \begin{cases} 1, & if \; \exists j, A_{cont_j}^i > Th_g \\ 0, & otherwise \end{cases}, \tag{4}$$

where $A_{cont_j}^i$ indicates the area of the *j-th* candidate object $Cont_j^i$ in the *i-th* image $I_i$. The geometric constrain threshold $Th_g$ is empirically set.

## 2.4 Fine- and Coarse-Grained Acceleration

In addition to module FRM and WRT are I/O-intensive operations, module MT and OBJ are computationally intensive operations, and are easy to accelerate. Module MT can be further divided into colorspace conversion (CVT), short time background image building (BUILD), long time background image updating (UPDAT), change detection (ChDet), and the morphology operation (Morph). Operation CVT, BUILD, UPDAT, and ChDet run in pixel-wise computation manner, which can be easily mapped into the Compute Unified Device Architecture (CUDA) [26] diagram by maximizing the use of grid, block, and thread parallelisms. Operation Morph is computed in a sliding window manner. Therefore, operation Morph is accelerated using more advanced techniques, such as texture, shared memory optimization and 2D convolutional kernel separation [26, 27]. The computation of module MT and OBJ are frame-independent, therefore we also implement module MT and OBJ using OpenMP [31] implementation to exploit frame-level parallelism. In OpenMP implementation, module MT and OBJ are assigned with $n_1$ and $n_2$ CPU threads respectively. When module MT is implemented using CUDA, we set $n_1$ to 1. We can split the long video into $K$ parts, and exploit task-level parallelism. These $K$ parts can be processed simultaneously, the processing time becomes shorter.

## 3 Platform-Adaptive CDVC System

In this section, we first discuss the computational resources assignment $(n_1, n_2, K)$ for a specific platform. Then we introduce the local search-based computational resources assignment, making the search of optimal assignment efficient. Finally, we introduce the proposed platform-adaptive CDVC system by using different combination of modules and different implementation of modules.

### 3.1 Brute Force-Based Computational Resources Assignment

To obtain a high-performance system, the computational resources assigned to coarse- and fine-grained accelerations should be balanced [29, 30, 32] which means a proper computational resource assignment $(n_1, n_2, K)$ is required to minimize the overall processing time. Taking OpenMP implementation of module MT and OBJ as an example. Module MT runs simultaneously with module FRM and OBJWRT, processing different interval of the buffered images. For a platform that has two CPUs and each of them has 8-cores, all possible assignments are listed in Table 1. The optimal assignment for this platform is (4, 4, 4), which is interpreted as four parts are running simultaneously, in each part modules MT and OBJ are assigned with four threads, respectively.

**Table 1.** Test time for different $(n_1, n_2, K)$ assignment on platform with GTX750Ti and E5-2650@2.0 GHz 8 cores × 2.

| K | 1 | | | | 2 | | | | 4 | | | |
|---|---|---|---|---|---|---|---|---|---|---|---|---|
| $n_2$ | $n_1$ | | | | $n_1$ | | | | $n_1$ | | | |
| | 1 | 2 | 4 | 8 | 1 | 2 | 4 | 8 | 1 | 2 | 4 | 8 |
| 1 | 150 | 114 | 126 | 118 | 107 | 80 | 73 | 70 | 56 | 42 | 42 | 42 |
| 2 | 148 | 108 | 102 | 108 | 107 | 76 | 65 | 64 | 52 | 39 | 37 | 39 |
| 4 | 151 | 126 | 85 | 91 | 109 | 76 | 61 | 63 | 60 | 41 | **36** | 38 |
| 8 | 156 | 109 | 92 | 91 | 110 | 74 | 54 | 55 | 54 | 40 | 37 | 38 |

## 3.2 Efficient Local Search-Based Computational Resources Assignment

Using brutal force search method, the number of all possible combinations of $(n_1, n_2, K)$ is $O(n^3)$, where $n$ is the maximum number of threads. It is unacceptable to find the assignment using brutal force search when $n$ is large. In the parameter selection domain [12, 13], the local search method is an alternative method and commonly used.

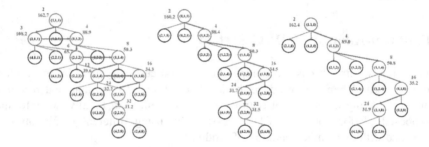

**Fig. 3.** Assignment searching trees for the mentioned three strategies. The circle represents one state $(n_1, n_2, K)$. The numbers beside the circle denote the resource used and processing time. The red bold arrow represents the state selected by the corresponding strategies.

In the local search method, an assignment $(n_1, n_2, K)$ is regarded as a state. The valid operation for a state is to increase the value of one element in $(n_1, n_2, K)$ if it is not beyond the valid range. We test each new state, and record its processing time and total computational resources used (equal to $(n_1 + n_2) \times K$). As shown in Fig. 3, the strategies we used to select one state among the new expanded states are as follows: (I) the minimal resource used first, (II) the minimal processing time first, and (III) regularizing the processing time performance improvement based on Strategy II. As shown in Table 1, the intuition of Strategy III is that adjacent assignments may achieve compatible performance (given the threshold of performance improvement, $Th_p$), which implies that we can stop expansion and test new states as early as possible. As shown in Table 1 and Fig. 3, the optimal computational resources assigned by Strategy III is different from those assigned by the other two strategies and brutal force search, but the run time performances of these assignments are nearly the same. For the search efficiency, the entire search time of local search method used Strategy III (about 13 min) is one order faster than that of brutal search method (about 141 min).

### 3.3 Platform-Adaptive Mechanism

In the data processing centers, various hardware configures may exist. To take full advantage of the platform computational resources, the combination and implementation of modules are also needed to be optimized, besides the optimal computational resources assignment. Hence, eight possible combination schemes are produced, i.e., A1, A2, A4, A6, B10, B12, C16 and C18, as shown in Fig. 4. The throughput performance comparison of different schemes is illuminated in Fig. 7 in bar plots.

Given a platform, we determine the optimal scheme from A1, A2, A4, A6, B10, B12, C16 and C18, each of which is with optimal computational resources assignment $(n_1, n_2, K)$. Although the overhead of the determination of the optimal combination and assignment exists, it just runs once for this platform. Therefore, the proposed CDVC system is efficiently platform-adaptive and is able to make full use of the computational resources.

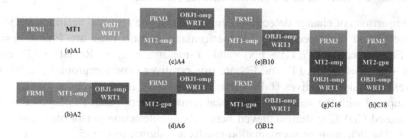

**Fig. 4.** Combination of modules FRM, MT and OBJWRT. The number following the module name is the number of the buffered images. Different number indicates different time interval of the buffered images. The "-omp" and "-gpu" are corresponding to OpenMP and CUDA implementation respectively.

## 4 Experiment and Analysis

Datasets provided by the IEEE Change Detection Workshop in conjunction with CVPR 2012 [28] (http://wordpress-jodoin.dmi.usherb.ca/dataset2012/) were used to validate the proposed CDVC system. In addition, ten outdoor surveillance video sequences, each of which lasted 30 min, were used. The details of the operating environment and the system setup are shown in Table 2.

To use less memory, $N_{sbg}$ (in Eq. (2)) was set to 100. To balance change detection accuracy and sensitivity to scene change, $N_{bg}$ (in Eq. (1)) was set to 2000. The change detection threshold $Th$ (in Eq. (3)) was set to 30. The area of connected component threshold $Th_g$ (in Eq. (4)) was set to 1600, and should be adjusted manually and carefully with respect to actual scene. To balance the efficiency and accuracy of computational resources assignment via the local search method, $Th_p$ (used in local

**Table 2.** Details of the running environment.

| | Platform GTX750Ti | Platform GTX550Ti |
|---|---|---|
| Hardware | CPU: 2.0 GHz 8 cores × 2<br>GPU: Nvidia GeForce GTX 550 Ti | CPU: 3.2 GHz 2 cores<br>GPU: Nvidia GeForce GTX 550 Ti |
| Operating system | Windows server 2008 R2 enterprise 64 bit | Windows 7 ultimate 64 bit |

search Strategy III) was set to 1 s. The maximum value of $K$ was set to eight to limit the parameter space. The maximum values of $n_1$ and $n_2$ were set to the maximum number of accessible threads. The values of $n_1$, $n_2$ and $K$ increased by the exponent of two.

The performance evaluation metric used in this study is throughput, which is defined as follows

$$throughput = file\ size/run\ time, \tag{5}$$

where the unit of file size is megabyte (MB), and the unit of the run time is second (s).

## 4.1    Change Detection and Frame Removal Accuracy

The comparisons of change detection accuracy and frame removal accuracy are shown in Tables 3 and 4, respectively. The performance metric used are Precision = TP/(TP + FP), Recall = TP/(TP + FN) and F-measure = 2 · Recall · Precision/(Recall + Precision). TP, FP, and FN are true positives (true foreground pixels), false positives, and false negatives (false background pixels), respectively.

Compared with the scale invariant local ternary pattern (SILTP) proposed in [10], the proposed CDVC system achieved better change detection performance, shown in Table 3. The detection or segmentation results are shown in Fig. 5.

For the proposed CDVC system, the accuracy of determining whether to keep a frame or not is high, as shown in Table 4. Change detection is conceptually simple, but is sufficient to detect moving or important activities. Therefore, a relative high accuracy of determining whether keeping a frame or not is achieved.

**Table 3.** Change detection accuracy comparison between the CDVC system and SILTP. The test video sequences were obtained from change detection 2012.

| Sequence | Precision | | Recall | | F-measure | |
|---|---|---|---|---|---|---|
| | CDVC | SILTP | CDVC | SILTP | CDVC | SILTP |
| Highway | 0.87 | 0.59 | 0.91 | 0.96 | 0.89 | 0.73 |
| Office | 0.70 | – | 0.74 | – | 0.72 | – |
| Pedestrians | 0.99 | 0.38 | 0.99 | 0.95 | 0.99 | 0.54 |
| PETS2006 | 0.86 | 0.54 | 0.72 | 0.97 | 0.78 | 0.70 |
| Average | 0.86 | 0.50 | 0.84 | 0.96 | 0.85 | 0.66 |

**Table 4.** Video condensation accuracy.

|  | Precision | Recall | F-measure |
|---|---|---|---|
| Highway | 1 | 1 | 1 |
| Office | 0.99 | 1 | 0.99 |
| Pedestrians | 1 | 0.78 | 0.88 |
| PETS2006 | 1 | 1 | 1 |

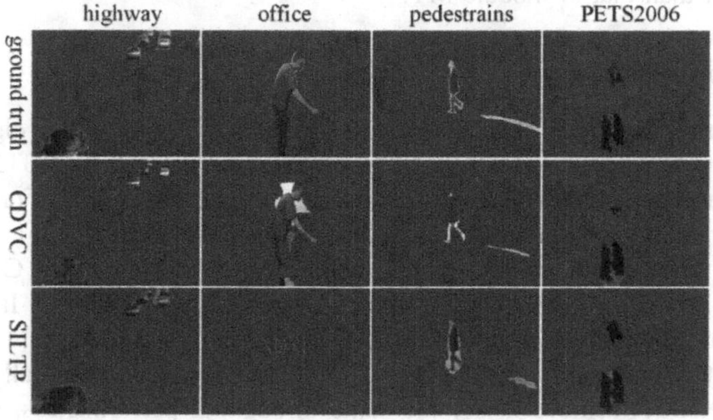

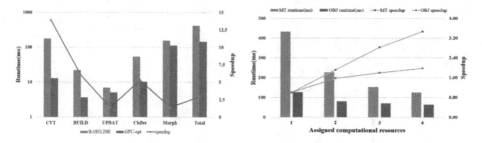

**Fig. 5.** Change detection results of CDVC and SILTP.

## 4.2 Speedup via Fine-Grained Acceleration

**GPU Acceleration.** GPU implementation of module MT on platform GTX550Ti is 2.9 times faster than CPU baseline setting $n_1$ to $1$[1], as shown in Fig. 6. The speedup of

**Fig. 6.** Module MT speedup performance of GPU acceleration compared with the single-thread CPU implementation (left). Runtime is plotted in logarithmic-form. Modules MT and OBJ speedup performances of multithreading acceleration compared with the single-thread CPU implementation (right).

---

[1] Note that speedup is hardware dependent, given better hardware may lead to better speedup performance. The overall speedup for platform GTX750Ti is 12.6.

operation CVT, BUILD, UPDAT, ChDet, and Morph are 13.9, 5.98, 1.38, 5.28, and 1.40, respectively.

**Multithreading Acceleration.** The speedup performance of module MT on platform GTX550Ti increases almost linearly with the increase in assigned computational resources and reaches 3.5, as shown in Fig. 6. By contrast, the speedup of module OBJ only reaches 2.0 when assigned with four threads. The difference of the speedup performances can be interpreted that connected component labeling in module OBJ is more complex than that of module MT.

### 4.3 Platform-Adaptive

Taking platform GTX550Ti as an example, the entire search time for all eight schemes of the three strategies is 2.2, 1.7 and 1.5 h as shown in Table 5. For GTX750Ti, the best scheme and computational resources assignment is C16 (2, 1, 8). For GTX550Ti the best scheme and computational resources assignment is A6 (1, 1, 4).

With the same fixed assignment, the throughput performance of GTX550Ti is compatible with that of GTX750Ti, as shown with bar graph in Fig. 7. It is the CPU frequency that plays an important role in the fixed assignment scenario.

In the best assignment scenario, as shown with line graph in Fig. 7, all schemes on platform GTX550Ti achieve nearly the same throughput performances, whereas the throughput performances on platform GTX750Ti vary considerably. It is the number of physical cores in CPU that plays an important role in the best assignment scenario.

**Table 5.** Number of expanded states of the three strategies.

| Strategy | A 1 | A 2 | A 4 | A 6 | B 10 | B 12 | C 16 | C 18 | Total | Time (h) |
|----------|-----|-----|-----|-----|------|------|------|------|-------|----------|
| I        | 3   | 13  | 15  | 8   | 15   | 9    | 11   | 6    | 80    | 2.2      |
| II       | 3   | 11  | 11  | 8   | 11   | 6    | 9    | 5    | 64    | 1.7      |
| III      | 3   | 9   | 9   | 6   | 9    | 7    | 9    | 5    | 57    | 1.5      |

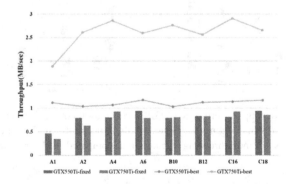

**Fig. 7.** The throughput performance with a fixed assignment is plotted in bar. The throughput performance with the best assignment is plotted in line.

## 4.4 Throughput Performance

Using the best assignment, we run the video condensation system to process the other ten surveillance video sequences. On platform GTX550Ti, the proposed system condensed one-hour videos @352 × 288 in about 60 s, and achieved 2.6 MB/s throughput. In terms of fps, for the video resolution of 704 × 576, platform GTX550Ti achieves 295.7 fps, whereas platform GTX750Ti achieves 730.9 fps. As reported in [10], the 8-core CPU @ 2.66 GHz and Nvidia GeForce GTX285 achieves 292.2 fps for the same video resolution. For the video resolution of 352 × 288, platform GTX550Ti achieves 1426.3 fps, whereas platform GTX750Ti achieves 3719 fps. As reported in [10], it achieves 833.6 fps for the same video resolution. The computational ability of GTX285 is slightly lower than that of GTX550Ti, whereas the computational ability of 8-core CPU @ 2.66 GHz is faster than that of 2-core CPU @ 3.20 GHz. Considering the platform characteristics, the results in this study is promising.

## 5 Conclusion

A platform-adaptive high-throughput performance video condensation system based on change detection is proposed in this study. The CDVC framework is accelerated using GPU and multithreading. To make full use of the computational resources, we resort to local search method to find the optimal assignment. To be platform-adaptive, we combine the modules of the proposed CDVC system to take advantage of module parallelism. Detailed experiments indicate that the proposed CDVC system is efficiently platform-adaptive for different hardware configurations and provides high throughput performance and high accuracy to keep important frames.

**Acknowledgements.** This work was supported in part by the Chinese National Natural Science Foundation Projects #U1435219, #61402507, #61572515, #61402499.

# References

1. O'callaghan, D., Lew, E.L.: Method and apparatus for video on demand with fast forward, reverse and channel pause, U.S. Patent 5 477 263, 19 December 1995
2. Smith, M.A.: Video skimming and characterization through the combination of image and language understanding techniques. In: Proceedings of the IEEE Conference on CVPR, 1997, pp. 775–781
3. Petrovic, N., Jojic, N., Huang, T.S.: Adaptive video fast forward. Multimed. Tools Appl. **26** (3), 327–344 (2005)
4. Hoferlin, B., Hoferlin, M., Weiskopf, D., Heidemann, G.: Information-based adaptive fast-forward for visual surveillance. Multimed. Tools Appl. **55**(1), 127–150 (2011)
5. Kang, H.-W., Chen, X.-Q., Matsushita, Y., Tang, X.: Space-time video montage. In: Proceedings of the IEEE Conference on CVPR, pp. 1331–1338 (2006)
6. Li, Z., Ishwar, P., Konrad, J.: Video condensation by ribbon carving. IEEE Trans. Image Process. **18**(11), 2572–2583 (2009)
7. Pritch, Y., Rav-Acha, A., Peleg, S.: Nonchronological video synopsis and indexing. IEEE Trans. Pattern Anal. Mach. Intell. **30**(11), 1971–1984 (2008)

8. Pritch, Y., Rav-Acha, A., Gutman, A., Peleg, S.: Webcam synopsis: peeking around the world. In: Proceedings of the IEEE ICCV, pp. 1–8 (2007)
9. Rav-Acha, A., Pritch, Y., Peleg, S.: Making a long video short: Dynamic video synopsis. In: Proceedings of the IEEE Conference on CVPR, pp. 435–441 (2006)
10. Zhu, J., Feng, S., Yi, D., Liao, S., Lei, Z., Li, S.Z.: High performance video condensation system, IEEE Trans. Circuits Syst. Video Technol. (2014)
11. Huang, C.-R., Chung, P.-C., Yang, D.-K., Chen, H.-C., Huang, G.-J.: Maximum a posteriori probability estimation for online surveillance video synopsis. IEEE Trans. Circuits Syst. Video Technol. 24(8), 1417–1429 (2014)
12. Hutter, F., Hoos, H.H., Leyton-Brown, K., Stutzle, T.: ParamILS: an automatic algorithm configuration framework. J. Artif. Intell. Res. 36(1), 267–306 (2009)
13. Xu, L., Hutter, F., Hoos, H.H., Leyton-Brown, K.: SATzilla: portfolio-based algorithms selection for SAT. J. Artif. Intell. Res. 32, 565–606 (2008)
14. Wren, C.R., Azarbayejani, A., Darrell, T., Pentland, A.P.: Pfinder: real-time tracking of the human body. IEEE Trans. Pattern Anal. Mach. Intell. 19(7), 780–785 (1997)
15. Koller, D., Weber, J., Huang, T., Malik, J., Ogasawara, G., Rao, B., Russel, S.: Toward robust automatic traffic scene analysis in real-time. In: Proceedings of the IEEE ICPR, pp. 126–131 (1994)
16. Friedman, N., Russell, S.: Image segmentation in video sequences: a probabilistic approach, In: Proceedings of the 13th Conference on Uncertainty in Artificial Intelligence, pp. 175–181 (1997)
17. Stauffer, C., Grimson, W.E.L.: Adaptive background mixture models for real-time tracking. In: Proceedings of the IEEE CVPR, pp. 246–252 (1999)
18. Hayman, E., Eklundh, J.: Statistical background subtraction for a mobile observer. In: Proceedings of the IEEE ICCV, pp. 67–74 (2003)
19. KaewTraKulPong, P., Bowden, R.: An improved adaptive background mixture model for real-time tracking with shadow detection. In: Proceedings of the European Workshop Advanced Video-Based Surveillance Systems, pp. 135–144 (2002)
20. Zivkovic, Z., der Heijden, E.: Recursive unsupervised learning of finite mixture models, IEEE Trans. Pattern Anal. Mach. Intell. 26(5) (2004)
21. Zivkovic, Z.: Improved adaptive gaussian mixture model for background subtraction. In: Proceedings of the IEEE ICPR, pp. 28–31 (2004)
22. Dubuisson, M.P., Jain, A.K.: Contour extraction of moving objects in complex outdoor scenes. Int. J. Comput. Vis. 14(1), 83–105 (1995)
23. Lipton, A.J., Fujiyoshi, H., Patil, R.S.: Moving target classification and tracking from real-time video. In: Proceedings of the IEEE Workshop on Applications of Computer Vision, pp. 8–14 (1998)
24. Suzuki, S., Abe, K.: Topological structural analysis of digitized binary images by border following. Comput. Vis. Graph. Image Process. 30(1), 32–46 (1985)
25. Teh, C.H., Chin, R.T.: On the detection of dominant points on digital curve. IEEE Trans. Pattern Anal. Mach. Intell. 11(8), 859–872 (1989)
26. Nvidia CUDA Programming Guide 2.0. http://www.nvidia.com/object/cuda_develop.html
27. Podlozhnyuk, V.: "Image Convolution with CUDA," Nvidia CUDA 2.0 SDK convolution Speparable document
28. Goyette, N., Jodoin, P.-M., Porikli, F., Konrad, J., Ishwar, P.: Changedetection.net: a new change detection benchmark dataset. In: Proceedings of the IEEE Workshop on Change Detection (CDW-2012) at CVPR-2012, Providence, RI, 16–21 June 2012
29. Wang, Y., Dou, Y., Guo, S., Lei, Y., Zou, D.: CPU–GPU hybrid parallel strategy for cosmological simulations. Concurr. Comput. Pract. Exp. 26(3), 748–765 (2014)

30. Lei, G., Dou, Y., Wan, W., Xia, F., Li, R., Ma, M., Zou, D.: CPU-GPU hybrid accelerating the Zuker algorithm for RNA secondary structure prediction applications, BMC Genomics **13**(Suppl 1) (2012)
31. Chandra, R.: Parallel Programming in OpenMP. Morgan Kaufmann, Burlington (2001)
32. Hermann, E., Raffin, B., Faure, F., et al.: Multi-GPU and multi-CPU parallelization for interactive physics simulations. In: Euro-Par 2010-Parallel Processing, pp. 235–246 (2010)

# Using Data Compression for Optimizing FPGA-Based Convolutional Neural Network Accelerators

Yijin Guan[1(✉)], Ningyi Xu[2], Chen Zhang[1], Zhihang Yuan[1],
and Jason Cong[1,3]

[1] Center for Energy-Efficient Computing and Applications, PKU, Beijing, China
guanyijin@pku.edu.cn
[2] Microsoft Research Asia, Beijing, China
[3] Computer Science Department, University of California, Los Angeles, USA

**Abstract.** Convolutional Neural Network (CNN) has been extensively employed in research fields including multimedia recognition, computer version, etc. Various FPGA-based accelerators for deep CNN have been proposed to achieve high energy-efficiency. For some FPGA-based CNN accelerators in embedded systems, such as UAVs, IoT, and wearable devices, their overall performance is greatly bounded by the limited data bandwidth to the on-board DRAM. In this paper, we argue that it is feasible to overcome the bandwidth bottleneck using data compression techniques. We propose an *effective roofline model* to explore design trade-off between computation logic and data bandwidth after applying data compression techniques to parameters of CNNs. We implement a decompression module and a CNN accelerator on a single Xilinx VC707 FPGA board with two different compression/decompression algorithms as case studies. Under a scenario with limited data bandwidth, the peak performance of our implementation can outperform designs using previous methods by 3.2× in overall performance.

**Keywords:** CNN · FPGA · Compression/decompression

## 1 Introduction

Convolutional Neural Network (CNN) [9], a popular deep learning algorithm, has become the most successful algorithm for visual content understanding, image search, and classification [6,8]. In recent years, CNN has achieved great improvement on both neural network architecture and accuracy, which makes CNN outperform conventional approaches. However, previous research has demonstrated that general purposed processors like CPUs are not efficient to perform the computation of CNN algorithms. As a result, various accelerators for CNN have been proposed recently. Among these accelerators, FPGA-based CNN accelerators have attracted great attention because of their high performance, low power consumption (compared with CPUs), and flexibility [1,5,10,11,16].

© Springer International Publishing AG 2017
Y. Dou et al. (Eds.): APPT 2017, LNCS 10561, pp. 14–26, 2017.
DOI: 10.1007/978-3-319-67952-5_2

Previous works on FPGA-based CNN accelerator aim at optimizing computation throughput [1,5,11] and I/O bandwidth [10] to achieve the best performance. In [16], Zhang et al. proposed a roofline model to find the design solution with the highest performance and lowest bandwidth requirements. The model can help find an optimal design configuration under the constraints of computation roof and bandwidth roof, which are provided by the specific hardware platform. More details can be found in Sect. 2.2.

Having this model, it is also easy to tell whether computation resource or I/O bandwidth has become the bottleneck of an FPGA-based CNN accelerator. In fact, in most of modern embedded systems, such as UAVs, mobile phones, IoT and wearable devices, the I/O bandwidth limitation (commonly 100–200 MB/s) is even stricter, which further lowers the bandwidth roof and results in a decrease on the overall performance of the CNN accelerators.

To overcome the problem of limited bandwidth, we further explore trade-off between computation resource and data bandwidth with consideration of compression techniques. In particular, we notice that the number of parameters (weights and bias) in real-life CNN is usually too large to be stored on-chip (e.g. about 60 million and 140 million of parameters for AlexNet [7] and VGG [12] respectively), which indicates that users need to load parameters from external storage to computation engines for CNN computation. Besides, the parameters of CNN are pre-calculated off-line in training phase, and they remain the same during inference phase. Taking advantage of this characteristic, we can compress these parameters off-line in advance, and only decompress them on-line on FPGA for CNN computation. While applied in embedded systems, CNN only performs the inference phase in various real-life applications, so we focus on a real-time acceleration for the inference phase of CNN.

To find the optimal design, we propose an effective roofline model. Consequently, we can further improve performance and even reduce energy consumption under the same bandwidth constraint. Moreover, we also provide analysis on the design space exploration and characteristics of different compression/decompression algorithms. To the best of our knowledge, this is the first work on applying compression/decompression methods to the parameters of CNN to improve the bandwidth bottleneck.

The main contributions of this work are summarized as follows,

- We build an effective roofline model for problem formulation and performance analysis, which takes both CNN accelerator and decompression module into consideration.
- We present a method to find the optimal configuration for architecture design, with a best on-chip resource allocation between CNN accelerator and decompression module using the effective roofline model.
- As case studies, we implement decompression modules using two typical compression/decompression algorithms, which improve the performance of CNN accelerator by 2.37× and 3.20× respectively, while saving energy at the same time.

The rest of this paper is organized as follows: Sect. 2 introduces CNN and roofline model, and Sect. 3 explains our methodology for performance optimization. Section 4 presents our hardware implementation. Experimental results and analysis are shown in Sect. 5. Section 6 concludes this paper and discusses about future work.

## 2 Background

In this section, we first introduce some basic concepts of CNN and explain our ideas generally. Then we present the roofline model for performance analysis in previous work.

### 2.1 CNN Basis

CNN is a classical supervised learning algorithm, and has achieved state-of-the-art accuracy across a broad set of applications. Typically, CNN is composed of two kinds of layers: convolutional layers (feature extractor) and fully connected layers (classifier).

A typical convolutional layer is shown in Fig. 1. As this figure illustrates, several feature maps form the input of a convolutional layer. These input feature maps are filtered by their own convolution kernels, then we can get a set of filtered feature maps as the output. Each convolution kernel is composed of many parameters, also called weights and bias. Deploying a CNN normally includes two phases: training and inference. In practice, training is accomplished off-line using a cluster of CPUs [4] or GPUs [2,14,15], and parameters are adjusted in a backward direction to get the best accuracy with a training set. During inference phase, the trained CNN is deployed for real-life applications, and computation executes in a forward direction on-line. So the speed of inference is the key factor of CNN's overall performance, and we focus on accelerating the inference phase in this work. It is worth noting that parameters remain unchanged during inference, which provides us with the possibility of compressing them off-line before they are applied to real-life applications, and only doing the decompression work on-line.

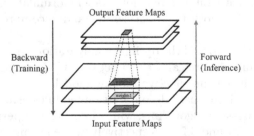

**Fig. 1.** Overview of a convolutional layer

Work in [3] has demonstrated that convolutional operations will occupy over 90% of the computation time of a CNN during the inference phase, so we focus on accelerating convolutional layers in this work, and discuss about fully connected layers in Sect. 6.

## 2.2  Roofline Model

Roofline Model is first introduced in [13] to restrict system performance under the highest attainable performance and data accessing bandwidth provided by a specific platform. Figure 2 shows an example of roofline model.

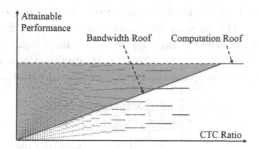

**Fig. 2.** Performance analysis using roofline model

As shown in Fig. 2, in roofline model, X-axis is computation to communication ratio (*CTC Ratio*), which indicates the number of computation operations per I/O traffic. Y-axis is the attainable performance (*AP*) of a design in GOPS (Giga operations per second). Here we denote the number of computation operations in CNN accelerator as *Operations*, and denote the amount of external data access for computation as *Data*. So we can calculate *CTC Ratio* and *AP* according to Eq. 1. According the definitions of *CTC Ratio* and *AP*, we can calculate the required bandwidth ($BW_r$) of a possible design by Eq. 2.

Roofline model defines computation roof to represent the peak performance that utilizes all the computation resources, and it also defines bandwidth roof, whose slope equals to the maximum data accessing bandwidth provided by the hardware platform (denoted by *BW*). On this hardware platform, the highest performance that the accelerator can achieve is restricted by computation roof and bandwidth roof. This can be summarized in Eq. 3.

$$CTC\ Ratio = \frac{Operations}{Data}, \quad AP = \frac{Opereations}{Cycles} \tag{1}$$

$$BW_r = \frac{Data}{Cycles} = \frac{AP}{CTC\ Ratio} \tag{2}$$

$$AP_{max} = min(Computation\ Roof,\ CTC\ Ratio * BW) \tag{3}$$

## 3    Methodology

### 3.1    Effective Roofline Model

Inspired by roofline model, we propose an effective roofline model for performance optimization. Applying decompression module to CNN accelerator brings some changes to the formulations in Sect. 2.2. We denote the compression ratio as $r$ (Eq. 4). For a single decompression unit, we denote its throughput as $BW_d$, which equals to the amount of data that the decompression unit can output in one second. However, a single decompression unit may not satisfy our demand for maximized resource utilization and higher performance, so we duplicate decompression unit according to the resources on chip, which offers great conciseness and flexibility to our adjustment of resource utilization and speed of decompression. Here we denote the number of duplications as $n$. In fact, the data size of input enoughignored when compared with the huge amount of parameters to be loaded during inference phase. So the Attainable Performance and CTC Ratio after applying a decompression module can be calculated by Eqs. 5 and 6 respectively.

$$r = \frac{Size\ of\ Compressed\ Data}{Size\ of\ Original\ Data} \qquad (4)$$

$$CTC\ Ratio' = \frac{Operations}{Data'} = \frac{Operations}{Data\ *\ r} \qquad (5)$$

$$AP' = \frac{Operations}{Cycles\ +\ Cycles\ of\ Decompression} = \frac{Opereations}{Cycles\ +\ \frac{Data}{n\ *\ BW_d}} \qquad (6)$$

To find the best design configuration under roofline model, we need to calculate the new locations of all the design points again every time the value of $n$ changes. As a result, the amount of overall computation for estimation is highly increased, which makes it more difficult to find the best design configuration. So we propose to solve this problem in another easier and clearer way.

According to Sect. 2.2, we denote the I/O bandwidth provided by the platform as $BW$. While applying a decompression module between storage and CNN accelerator, the I/O bandwidth that the CNN accelerator actually obtains varies, we denote it as $BW'$. Based on the definitions above, the relationship between $BW'$ and $BW$ is shown in Eqs. 7 and 8. $BW$ is determined by the specific platform. $r$ and $BW_d$ are determined by the compression/decompression algorithms and hardware implementations respectively. $n$ is the variant to reflect the trade-off between resources for decompression module and resources for CNN accelerator.

$$When\ n = 0,\ BW' = BW \qquad (7)$$

$$When\ n > 0,\ BW' = \frac{BW}{r\ +\ \frac{BW}{n\ *\ BW_d}} \qquad (8)$$

With the formulations above, we present an effective roofline model to solve the highly complex problem that the decompression module brings.

Figure 3 shows an example of our effective roofline model. In effective roofline model, we define an effective computation roof ($ECR$) as the highest attainable performance of CNN accelerator with the on-chip resources that can be used for it, and we also define an effective bandwidth roof ($EBR$), whose slope equals to $BW'$.

Deploying a decompression module has two aspects of influence on the CNN accelerator: On the one hand, the decompression module definitely occupies a certain amount of resources, which may decrease the on-chip resources available for CNN accelerator. As $n$ increases, the resources for CNN accelerator may further decrease, which results in a decrease on the attainable performance. This can be reflected as a downwards movement of $ECR$. On the other hand, according to Eq. 8, $BW'$ will increase when $n$ increases, which results in a anticlockwise movement of $EBR$ in effective roofline model. Therefore, for different choices of values for $n$ ($n_0 < n_1 < n_2$), the corresponding $ECR$s and $EBR$s are shown in Fig. 3.

As a result, the design space of the roofline model introduced in [16] is just a subset (when $n = 0$) of the design space of effective roofline model. After adding the decompression module, our effective roofline model takes computation power, bandwidth requirements and on-chip resource allocation into consideration, so it can explore a much larger design space and probably find a design configuration with better overall performance.

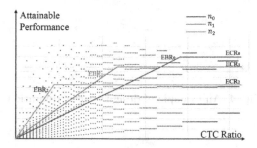

**Fig. 3.** An example of effective roofline model

## 3.2   Design Space Exploration

Taking advantage of the characteristics and parameterization of CNN accelerator, every possible design can be represented as a point in the effective roofline model. All these points comprise a huge space of possible design choices, and we propose a method to efficiently find the design with highest overall performance.

According to our effective roofline model, when $n$ equals to an arbitrary value, the method to find the best design configuration is similar to that in conventional roofline model. Under the constraints of $ECR$ and $EBR$, we can use a traversal approach to find the optimal configuration for architecture design with highest performance and lowest bandwidth requirements, and this method has been presented in [16]. Every time $n$ changes, $ECR$ and $EBR$ will change, which means that we need to search for the best design among all the points in all possible values of $n$. To simplify this procedure, we use pruning methods to shrink the searching space.

On the one hand, when $n = 0$, which means we do not apply decompression module to the CNN accelerator, we have $BW' = BW$. Using the method provided in [16], we can find a point (X in Fig. 4) with the best performance. Then we add decompression module to this system to search for a point with better overall performance. So if there exists such a point that is better than X, this point must be located at the left side of $EBR_{n=0}$ and at the upside of X's attainable performance. On the other hand, when we increase $n$ to further improve bandwidth bottleneck, $ECR$ may move downwards. Supposing $ECR$ equals to X's attainable performance when $n$ equals to a certain value (denoted by $n_{max}$), then there is no need to further increase $n$. Above all, we need to traverse $n$ from 1 to $n_{max}$ to search for the best trade-off in resource allocation. For each value of $n$, we only need to search for the best design among the points in the shaded region (shown in Fig. 4) instead of the entire design space.

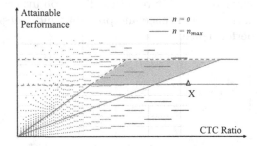

**Fig. 4.** An example of design space exploration

## 4    Implementation

### 4.1    System Design

The system design is shown in Fig. 5. We divide the whole function of this system into two parts: Compression and CNN-D (CNN accelerator with decompression module). The arrows in Fig. 5 show the direction of parameter flow. White arrows indicate that the parameters transferred are compressed, while black arrows indicate that the parameters transferred are decompressed.

As Fig. 5 illustrates, Compression is mainly implemented on software. The Compression Module is used to compress the parameters of our implemented CNN, and Dispatcher is deployed to dispatch them into the format suitable for parallel decompression. To emulate the bandwidth bounded scenario in embedded systems, we attach a NAND Flash chip to our FPGA board, and this NAND Flash chip works as the external storage where the parameters of CNN are stored.

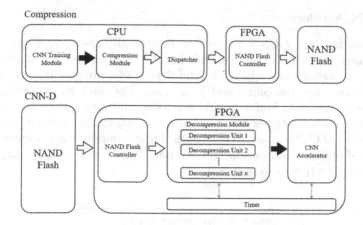

**Fig. 5.** Overview of system design

Our whole design of CNN-D is implemented on a single FPGA board. The NAND Flash Controller works as a data fetcher and data dispatcher for Decompression Module. It fetches parameters stored in the NAND Flash and dispatches parameters to each Decompression Unit. The Decompression Module is composed of $n$ Decompression Units, and each Decompression Unit decompresses the parameters transfered into it. After decompression, the decompressed parameters are transfered to the CNN Accelerator, where the main part of CNN computation is performed. What is more, we use a Timer to measure the execution time of our design.

## 4.2   Compression/Decompression Algorithms

Applying compression/decompression modules to minimize the amount of data to be transfered is a common approach in system design for bandwidth optimization. However, there is something different for our demand on the compression/decompression algorithms. Firstly, we do not care how much time and resources it costs to compress parameters of CNN, since we compress them offline only once, and store them in a read-only mode. Secondly, we hope decompression does not cost much time and resources considering the performance of the whole CNN accelerator. In summary, our requirements to the compression/decompression algorithms are: high compression ratio, high decompression speed and low resource utilization for decompression. Considering representativeness and our requirements, we choose LZ77 as an example of dictionary based algorithms, and Huffman Encoding as an example of entropy encoding based algorithms. Many compression/decompression algorithms used nowadays are variants or combinations of these two algorithms.

### 4.3   CNN Accelerator

The implementation of CNN accelerator is generally shown in Fig. 6. All the computation of CNN are accomplished in parallel by numerous convolution units. Several optimizations are applied to the design of convolution units, such as deep pipelining, loop unrolling and loop tiling. For data access optimization, we implement two data buffers for data reusing and ping-pong operations. All these optimization strategies can be parameterized, which makes it possible to calculate the *CTC Ratio* and *AP* of each design configuration accurately. For the choice of optimization parameters, we refer to the best design configuration found by our effective roofline model.

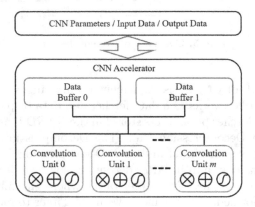

**Fig. 6.** Overview of CNN accelerator

## 5   Case Study

In this section, the experimental setup of our experiments is provided first. Then we present and analyze the experimental results.

### 5.1   Experimental Setup

We use Vivado HLS (v2015.4) to implement our CNN accelerator and decompression module. Vivado HLS is a high level synthesis design tool, which takes C code as input and outputs IP core in Verilog HDL. For the design space exploration and performance estimation, we use the pre-synthesis report of Vivado HLS. Then the RTL synthesis and implementation are done in Vivado (v2015.4).

The hardware platform we choose is a VC707 board with a Xilinx Virtex7 485t FPGA chip on it, and its working frequency is set to be 100 MHz. The storage device we use is SAMSUNG K9F1G08U0D NAND Flash board.

To test our effective roofline model in a real-life case, we implement a CNN with our accelerators, VGG-19 [12], which has 16 convolutional layers. The VGG

Model increases depth using an architecture with very small ($3 \times 3$) convolution kernels, which shows that a significant improvement on the prior-art configurations can be achieved by pushing the depth to 16–19 layers. The detailed configurations of VGG-19 can be found in [12]. The input is a $224 \times 224$ RGB image, and the convolution kernel size in convolutional layers is $3 \times 3$, with a sliding stride of 1.

## 5.2 Experimental Results

Table 1 shows the average compression ratio ($r$ in Sect. 3.1, $r < 1$), speed of decompression ($BW_d$ in Sect. 3.1) and resource utilization of different decompression units. From Table 1 we can see that Huffman Encoding performs about $1.30\times$ better than LZ77 on average compression ratio. This is because that LZ77 is a dictionary-based compression algorithm, and performs better when the data has a stronger locality. However, parameters of VGG-19 show a weak locality. In other CNN models, the locality of parameters varies, LZ77 may perform better. This is also the reason why we implement two different typical compression algorithms. According to analysis in Sect. 3.1, decompression speed of a single decompression unit is not very important for our application, since we can adjust $n$ for different $BW'$, and CNN computation is the dominating factor. As shown in Table 1, a single decompression unit does not occupy much resource. More specifically, the main kind of resource these decompression units occupy is LUT, and they do not use DSP at all. While computation resource (DSP) is crucial to the performance of CNN accelerator, so this means a greater space for our optimization.

**Table 1.** Decompression unit comparison

| Algorithm | $r$ | $BW_d$ | DSP | BRAM | LUT | FF |
|-----------|-----|--------|-----|------|-----|-----|
| LZ77 | 0.48 | 114.7 MB/s | 0.00% | 0.97% | 4.52% | 0.82% |
| Huffman | 0.37 | 90.61 MB/s | 0.00% | 0.49% | 1.04% | 0.16% |

We implement three cases for our studies: design with no decompression module (named as $CNN$), design combined with LZ77 decompression module (named as $CNN - D(LZ)$) and design combined with Huffman Encoding decompression module (named as $CNN - D(HE)$). All implementations implement the best hardware configuration found by the method presented in Sect. 3.2. The bandwidth of data accessing is 181.20 MB/s, which is within the typical bandwidth range (100–200 MB/s) in real-life embedded systems.

The overall resource utilization of these three designs are shown in Table 2. As shown in Table 1, decompression units occupy much more LUT and FF than DSP and BRAM. When we duplicate decompression units to achieve better performance, the demand for LUT and FF increases greatly. As a result, compared with $CNN$ in Table 2, we can observe a significant increase on the utilization of LUT and FF in $CNN - D(LZ)$ and $CNN - D(HE)$.

**Table 2.** Overall resource utilization

| Implementation | DSP | BRAM | LUT | FF |
|---|---|---|---|---|
| $CNN$ | 10.00% | 6.25% | 8.66% | 5.23% |
| $CNN - D(LZ)$ | 27.14% | 17.48% | 85.36% | 32.78% |
| $CNN - D(HE)$ | 40.00% | 30.10% | 89.92% | 18.39% |

**Table 3.** Performance comparison

| Number of layer | $CNN$ | | $CNN - D(LZ)$ | | $CNN - D(HE)$ | |
|---|---|---|---|---|---|---|
| | Time (s) | GOPS | Time (s) | GOPS | Time (s) | GOPS |
| 1 | 0.061 | 5.69 | 0.031 | 11.19 | 0.031 | 11.19 |
| 2 | 1.31 | 5.65 | 0.66 | 11.21 | 0.65 | 11.38 |
| 3 | 0.49 | 7.55 | 0.16 | 23.12 | 0.16 | 23.12 |
| 4 | 0.98 | 7.55 | 0.33 | 22.42 | 0.33 | 22.42 |
| 5 | 0.41 | 9.02 | 0.16 | 23.12 | 0.082 | 45.11 |
| 6, 7, 8 | 0.82 | 9.02 | 0.33 | 22.42 | 0.16 | 46.24 |
| 9 | 0.37 | 10.00 | 0.16 | 23.12 | 0.12 | 30.83 |
| 10, 11, 12 | 0.73 | 10.14 | 0.33 | 22.42 | 0.24 | 30.83 |
| 13, 14, 15, 16 | 0.18 | 10.07 | 0.082 | 22.55 | 0.061 | 30.21 |
| Overall GOPS | 8.66 | | 20.49 | | 27.69 | |
| Speedup | 1.00× | | 2.37× | | 3.20× | |

The performance comparison is shown in Table 3. Since the configurations of some convolutional layers in VGG-19 are the same, their results are shown in a single row. We show the results of convolutional layers only, because convolutional operations occupy most of the computation time of a CNN during the inference phase, which has been discussed about in Sect. 2.1.

The overall performance of $CNN$ is only 8.66 GOPS, which is pretty bad if compared with previous designs. For example, design in [16] can achieve an higher overall performance of 61.62 GOPS. However, it is worth noticing that the bandwidth roof of data accessing in $CNN$ is limited to 181.20 MB/s, which is within the typical bandwidth range (100–200 MB/s) in real-life embedded systems, while in design of [16], the bandwidth roof is 4.5 GB/s. So the obvious difference of overall performance proves our claim that limited bandwidth in embedded systems becomes a strict bound that prevents CNN accelerator from achieving a higher performance.

Compared with $CNN$, we can see that $CNN - D(LZ)$ achieves 2.37× speedup in overall performance, and the speedup that $CNN - D(HE)$ achieves is 3.20×. Since the change of runtime power of our FPGA board due to changes of resource utilization is slight enough to be ignored, we can save almost the same ratio of energy as that of speedups.

# 6 Conclusions and Future Work

In this paper, we propose to use data compression to further improve the overall performance of FPGA-based CNN accelerators. We present an effective roofline model to solve the resource trade-off between decompression module and CNN accelerator. This effective roofline model formulates a more general scenario and includes the design space of former CNN accelerator works. In addition, we shrink the design space for exploration, and provides a method to find the optimal design configuration. Finally, we implement the system on a Xilinx VC707 FPGA board, which achieved great improvement upon implementations using previous methods.

We are working on extension of this work in several directions. First of all, we use LZ77 and Huffman Encoding in our case studies. Lossy compression/decompression algorithms are not taken into consideration. We expect that, in the near future, we can come up with an accurate model to describe the key characteristics of different compression/decompression algorithms. What is more, this model can be combined with our effective roofline model for a better modeling and estimation. Secondly, Artificial Neural Network (ANN) is composed of fully connected layers only, which indicates more parameters to be transfered. Though the computation pattern of ANN is a little different from that of CNN, our proposed effective roofline model can still work with a few modifications. We plan to analyze several real-life ANNs applied in embedded systems, and test how much improvement we can achieve with the help of effective roofline model.

# References

1. Cadambi, S., Majumdar, A., Becchi, M., Chakradhar, S., Graf, H.P.: A programmable parallel accelerator for learning and classification. In: Proceedings of the 19th International Conference on Parallel Architectures and Compilation Techniques, pp. 273–284. ACM (2010)
2. Coates, A., Huval, B., Wang, T., Wu, D., Catanzaro, B., Andrew, N.: Deep learning with COTS HPC systems. In: Proceedings of the 30th International Conference on Machine Learning, pp. 1337–1345 (2013)
3. Cong, J., Xiao, B.: Minimizing computation in convolutional neural networks. In: Wermter, S., Weber, C., Duch, W., Honkela, T., Koprinkova-Hristova, P., Magg, S., Palm, G., Villa, A.E.P. (eds.) ICANN 2014. LNCS, vol. 8681, pp. 281–290. Springer, Cham (2014). doi:10.1007/978-3-319-11179-7_36
4. Dean, J., Corrado, G., Monga, R., Chen, K., Devin, M., Mao, M., Senior, A., Tucker, P., Yang, K., Le, Q.V., et al.: Large scale distributed deep networks. In: Advances in Neural Information Processing Systems, pp. 1223–1231 (2012)
5. Farabet, C., Poulet, C., Han, J.Y., LeCun, Y.: CNP: an FPGA-based processor for convolutional networks. In: International Conference on Field Programmable Logic and Applications, FPL 2009, pp. 32–37. IEEE (2009)
6. Ji, S., Xu, W., Yang, M., Yu, K.: 3D convolutional neural networks for human action recognition. IEEE Trans. Pattern Anal. Mach. Intell. **35**(1), 221–231 (2013)

7. Krizhevsky, A., Sutskever, I., Hinton, G.E.: ImageNet classification with deep convolutional neural networks. In: Advances in Neural Information Processing Systems, pp. 1097–1105 (2012)
8. Larochelle, H., Erhan, D., Courville, A., Bergstra, J., Bengio, Y.: An empirical evaluation of deep architectures on problems with many factors of variation. In: Proceedings of the 24th International Conference on Machine Learning, pp. 473–480. ACM (2007)
9. LeCun, Y., Bottou, L., Bengio, Y., Haffner, P.: Gradient-based learning applied to document recognition. Proc. IEEE **86**(11), 2278–2324 (1998)
10. Peemen, M., Setio, A., Mesman, B., Corporaal, H., et al.: Memory-centric accelerator design for convolutional neural networks. In: IEEE 31st International Conference on Computer Design (ICCD), pp. 13–19. IEEE (2013)
11. Sankaradas, M., Jakkula, V., Cadambi, S., Chakradhar, S., Durdanovic, I., Cosatto, E., Graf, H.P.: A massively parallel coprocessor for convolutional neural networks. In: 20th IEEE International Conference onApplication-specific Systems, Architectures and Processors, ASAP 2009, pp. 53–60. IEEE (2009)
12. Simonyan, K., Zisserman, A.: Very deep convolutional networks for large-scale image recognition. arXiv preprint arXiv:1409.1556 (2014)
13. Williams, S., Waterman, A., Patterson, D.: Roofline: an insightful visual performance model for multicore architectures. Commun. ACM **52**(4), 65–76 (2009)
14. Yadan, O., Adams, K., Taigman, Y., Ranzato, M.: Multi-GPU training of convnets. arXiv preprint arXiv:1312.5853, p. 17 (2013)
15. Yu, K.: Large-scale deep learning at Baidu. In: Proceedings of the 22nd ACM International Conference on Conference on Information and Knowledge Management, pp. 2211–2212. ACM (2013)
16. Zhang, C., Li, P., Sun, G., Guan, Y., Xiao, B., Cong, J.: Optimizing FPGA-based accelerator design for deep convolutional neural networks. In: Proceedings of the 2015 ACM/SIGDA International Symposium on Field-Programmable Gate Arrays, pp. 161–170. ACM (2015)

# Molecular Docking Simulation Based on CPU-GPU Heterogeneous Computing

Jinyan Xu, Jianhua Li$^{(\boxtimes)}$, and Yining Cai

Department of Computer Science and Engineering,
East China University of Science and Technology, Shanghai, China
jhli@ecust.edu.cn

**Abstract.** Receptor-ligand molecular docking aims to predict possible drug candidates for many diseases, and it requires a lot of computing cost. Shortening this time- consumption process will help pharmaceutical scientist to speed up drug development. In this paper, a parallel molecular docking simulation based on CPU-GPU heterogeneous computing is proposed. This simulation is developed from our previous developed molecular docking code iFitDock (Induced fit docking program) which introduced Non-dominated Sorting Genetic Algorithm II (NSGA II) and Molecular Mechanical-Generalized Born Surface Area (MM-GBSA) binding free energy. In this program, the most computationally intensive part is the computing of scoring functions due to complex computing process of free binding free energy. Thus, this paper focuses on offloading the computing of scoring functions as well as related conformation spatial transformation to GPU, and keeping the rest of the simulation on CPU. A detailed CPU-GPU heterogeneous computing model is constructed to parallelize the computing of scoring functions and related workload on the GPU and to define the data exchange between GPU and CPU. The primary parallel iFitDock system with only parallel semi-flexible docking implemented achieves a speedup of around $\sim 20\times$ with respect to a single CPU core. The result shows that it is very productive to use CPU-GPU heterogeneous computing for semi-flexible molecule docking cases in iFitDock.

**Keywords:** Molecular docking · Scoring function · CPU-GPU heterogeneous computing

## 1  Introduction

Receptor-ligand molecular docking is a process of achieving low energy stable complexes from two or more molecules through geometrical and energy matching in modern structure-based drug design. Computer simulation of molecular docking is a complex computing process to find out a set of low-energy molecule conformations. Typically, these low-energy conformations are searched and assessed by means of different reasonable and effective optimization methods, including Genetic Algorithm (GA), Fast Fourier Transform (FFT) correlations, Monte Carlo (MC) techniques, simulated annealing *etc.* [1–3].

The simulation of molecular docking always requires an intensive computing consumption. Besides that, docking quality depends on the coverage of the search

© Springer International Publishing AG 2017
Y. Dou et al. (Eds.): APPT 2017, LNCS 10561, pp. 27–37, 2017.
DOI: 10.1007/978-3-319-67952-5_3

space, which can be improved by increasing the number of random samples. Therefore, a fast and high-quality simulation is productive for molecular docking. Generally, parallelization of the simulation is a regular and efficient way to achieve this goal and some research work has been carried out. There are three categories of parallelization in literatures. The first category is parallel simulation based on a massively parallel system. For example, DOCK6.0 was used for high throughput computing validation on a massively parallel system IBM BlueGene. The second one is parallelization on Graphic Processing Units (GPUs) which is very popular and low-cost [4, 5]. Evaluation of the induced-fit effect [4, 5], Dock6's Amber Scoring [6], and genetic algorithm [7] were three typical parallelization objects on GPU. The third one is constructed on a reconfiguration hardware, e.g. field programmable gate array (FPGA) were chosen to speed up rigid-molecule docking [8]. However, the above researches are limited to their own applications, and the parallelization of molecular docking still needs to be further investigated.

In this paper, we focus on accelerating a specific docking program, Induced Fit Dock (iFitDock), which was developed by Bai *et al.* [9]. The serial version of iFitDock introduces multi-objective optimization algorithm NSGA II and Molecular Mechanical-Generalized Born Surface Area (MM-GBSA) binding free energy. As the number of conformations and that of populations grow, the workload of the program increases rapidly. Thus, there is a strong demand for a faster and more efficient iFitDock. In this paper, a new molecular docking simulation based on CPU-GPU heterogeneous computing is put forward. In this simulation, a CPU-GPU heterogeneous computing model is constructed and a primary parallel simulation system is implemented in Compute Unified Device Architecture (CUDA).

## 2   iFitDock - A Flexible Docking Program

### 2.1   Overview and Description of iFitDock

The docking program iFitDock has been developed to accurately predict the binding conformations for ligands to proteins (receptors), and to characterize the water molecules mediated binding interaction of drugs to their proteins. According to the different flexibilities for both ligands and proteins, iFitDock provides three docking modes: semi-flexible docking, flexible docking and key loop flexible docking. All modes have a similar computing procedure. Here, considering that the mode of semi-flexible docking is the simplest, the semi-flexible docking block is chosen as the parallelization object.

As a molecular docking program, iFitDock definitely includes the implementation of conformation search and conformation assessment, as shown in Fig. 1. Generally, conformation search refers to conformation sampling of ligand molecule and receptor molecule, and conformation assessment indicates evaluating and calculating of searched conformation. In the implementation of conformation search of this program, both the ligand and the receptor conformation change because of "induced-fit" effect. In the implementation of semi-flexible docking, the conformation assessment contains two objective functions, and they are:

(1) the sum of both the van der Waals energy and the electrostatic potential energy between small molecule and receptor protein.

(2) the sum of both the van der Waals energy and electrostatic potential energy among the atoms of the molecule.

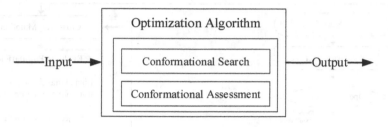

**Fig. 1.** Overview of the iFitDock program.

Both the objective functions can be calculated by the formula (1).

$$E = \sum_{i=1}^{I} \left[ \sqrt{A_{ii}} * \sum_{j=1}^{J} \frac{\sqrt{A_{jj}}}{r_{ij}^{12}} - \sqrt{B_{ii}} * \sum_{j=1}^{J} \frac{\sqrt{B_{jj}}}{r_{ij}^{6}} + 332.0 * q_i * \sum_{j=1}^{J} \frac{q_j}{D * r_{ij}} \right] \quad (1)$$

In this formula, $E$ is the interaction energy between the ligand and the receptor; $r_{ij}$ is the distance between the atom $i$ and the atom $j$; $A_{ij}$ and $B_{ij}$ are van der Waals exclusion and attracting parameters; $q_i$ and $q_j$ are the partial charges on the atom $i$ and the atom $j$; $D$ is the dielectric constant.

Considering that the conformation assessment is a multi-objective optimization problem, a multi-objective optimization algorithm (NSGA II) has been chosen to solve the docking simulation in iFitDock [10]. The main cycle process of the algorithm NSGA II is outlined as:

(1) Merge the parent population and the progeny population;

(2) Sort the merged population by non-domination sorting method;

(3) The first $i$-th rank individuals are incorporated into the new parent population until the parent population cannot be filled with the next rank individuals;

(4) Compute crowding-distance and sort by the crowding-comparison operator of each individual with $(i + 1)$-th rank;

(5) Incorporate the first N individuals into the new parent population until the parent population is full;

(6) Individuals in the parent population carry on crossover, mutation and selection to produce a new progeny population.

After introducing NSGA II, conformation search becomes the process of population initialization and transformation, while conformation assessment is still the computing process of the objective functions.

iFitDock divides the sampling space discretely for achieving a comprehensive and systematic drug-target binding mode, but the computation is intensive with fine meshing. In iFitDock, the detailed flowchart of semi-flexible docking within one single sampling space is illustrated in Fig. 2. Users can use Python to call the program to compute all the binding free energy of the entire sampling space in batch, and to result in a final conformation.

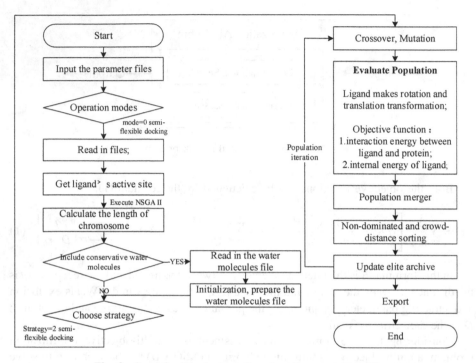

**Fig. 2.** Semi-flexible docking flowchart in one single grid

## 2.2    Time Expenditure of Serial iFitDock

Typically, offloading the most computationally intensive part of the serial program to the GPU is a common parallel strategy. Hence, the times expenditures of the serial iFitDock should be analyzed to find out which part is the most computationally intensive.

In this paper, a Urokinase Protein and a molecule C18H15N3O (6-[(Z)-AMINO (IMINO)METHYL]-N-PHENYL-2-NAPHTHAMIDE) are taken as inputs of iFit-Dock. When the population size is 2000 and the iteration is 350 generations, the semi-flexible docking of one single grid is tested and all the time expenditures of software modules in the program are recorded. Considering that the algorithm is a heuristic algorithm, the time consumptions have slight deviations among repeated experiments, and all the recorded values are the average of 10 experiments.

According to the functions of the program, there are six modules in this program, and their time expenditures are shown in Table 1. As can be seen from the Table 1, the total expenditure is about 2625 s. Among these six modules, the most time-consumption module is the second objective function and its time expenditure is about 2100 s, and the second most time-consumption module is the first objective function. The sum of the time expenditures of two objective functions reaches up to 87% of the total time due to complex computing process of free binding free energy. Moreover, the time expenditures of the rotation and translation, which belongs to the conformation search, takes the fourth palace in time expenditures. This statistical result in Table 1 shows that most computationally intensive parts of the program are the two scoring functions.

**Table 1.** Time expenditures of iFitDock

| Software module | Time | Total time |
| --- | --- | --- |
| I/O | 4.3 s | 2625 s |
| Mutation, crossover, sorting, *etc.* | 35 s | |
| Rotation and translation | 140 s | |
| The first objective function | 175 s | |
| The second objective function | 2100 s | |
| Other | 170 s | |

## 3   CPU-GPU Heterogeneous Model of Semi-flexible Docking

Based on the above statistical result, a CPU-GPU heterogeneous computing model is constructed to offload the computing of scoring functions as well as related confor-mation spatial transformation to GPU, as shown in Fig. 3. This model ensures that the data stream from random search method is the same in both CPU-only model and CPU-GPU model. The model consists of three parts: the program in CPU, the program in GPU, and the exchange data between CPU and GPU. The program in CPU not only deals with input data and output data, but also handles the crossover, mutation, merging, sorting and updating the elite file steps of the NSGA II. In addition, the program in CPU also handles the judgment and accumulation in objective functions. The exchange data between CPU and GPU are mainly the spatial coordinate values of all atoms, energy lattice values, the van der Waals energy and electrostatic potential energy between atoms. The program in GPU is divided into three parts:

(1) Computing three-dimensional transformation of small molecule and three-dimensional transformation around rotatable bonds of molecule internal atoms;
(2) Computing interaction energy between the small molecule and the protein;
(3) Computing internal energy of the small molecule.

The program in GPU is in charge of distributing the workload to threads, *i.e.* assigning detailed data to different threads, in this CPU-GPU heterogeneous computation. After the data being copied into GPU, the program in GPU computes the three-dimensional transformation of entire molecule and three-dimensional transformation around rotatable

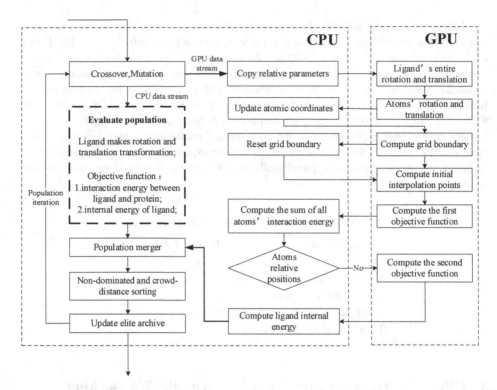

**Fig. 3.** CPU-GPU heterogeneous computing model

bonds of atoms. The kernel function of these two rotation transformations defines $16 \times 16$ threads in per block, each grid contains $(3 \times$ atom number $\times$ population size) $\div$ (dimBlock.x $\times$ dimBlock.y) blocks. Thus, each thread can compute the atomic coordinate values in each individual. After that, the coordinate values are backed up in CPU side. The program in GPU keeps on computing the energy grid boundary, and the program in CPU determines and resets the boundary, then the program in GPU computes interpolation points.

While computing the first objective function, namely, the computation of interaction energy between small molecule and protein, the program in GPU sets the threads in per block to the number of molecule atoms, each grid size is equal to the population size, so each thread can compute interaction energy between molecule and protein of each individual. The result returns to CPU for computing the sum of energy values. At the same time, the program in CPU removes non-computational atom pairs.

The second objective function in GPU is to compute the molecule's internal energy, it is the main time-consumption part in the original serial program. The kernel function of GPU sets the threads in per block to the number of atom pairs, each grid size is equal to the population size, so each thread can compute the energy of each individual's atom pair.

Finally, the program in CPU accumulates small molecule's internal energy.

## 4  Experimental Results and Analysis

The parallel version of iFitDock is developed under the mixed language of C++ and CUDA under Linux (Red Hat Enterprise release 5.8) operating system, and the test experiment is executed in a CPU-GPU heterogeneous computer whose configurations are shown in Table 2.

**Table 2.** Specification of CPU-GPU heterogeneous computer

|  | CPU | GPU |
|---|---|---|
| Hardware | intel(R) Xeon(R) CPU E5- 2650 @ 2.00 GHz | Tesla M2090 |
| CPU MHz | 2000.06 MHz |  |
| Computing power |  | 2.0 |
| CPU cores | 8 |  |
| CUDA version |  | 5.0 |
| Compiler version | gcc 6.2.0 | nvcc 5.0 |

Taking Urokinase Protein's semi-flexible docking as an example, when the population size is set to 2000, after running iterations of 350 generation, the conformations of docking results in a single grid are shown in Fig. 4. The colorful part is the final computed 20 conformation results. After running iteration of one generation with 2000 population size in the parallel program, we have figured out the time-consumption of CPU, GPU and memory copy for seven times, and results are shown in Fig. 5.

The serial program (denoted as "CPU" in Fig. 5) takes about 7.3 s by average when the population size is set to 2000 after running iterations of 350 generation, while parallel program (denoted as "GPU" in Fig. 5) in CPU-GPU heterogeneous computing only takes about 0.5 s by average. The parallel program is 14.6 times faster than the serial program. Therefore, computational efficiency has been greatly improved. The

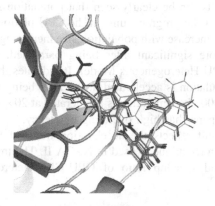

**Fig. 4.** Conformations of docking results in a single grid

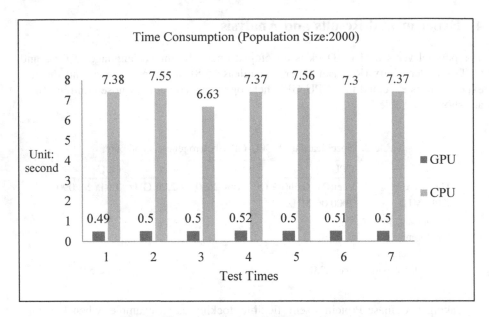

**Fig. 5.** Time consumption of 2000 population size

size of the population is an essential factor that affects the computation time significantly. The performance of our program is also tested in different inputted population size. When the population size reaches 1000, 2000, 3000, 4000 and 5000, we compute the time consumption within the iteration of one generation. The algorithm is performed only on CPU or on CPU-GPU heterogeneous model) separately for six times. The averages of results are shown in Fig. 6. Figure 7 shows the time-consumption of GPU calculation and its memory copy in the corresponding population size. The results show that the memory copy is growing slowly along with the population size growing, while the rest of the computation time grows relatively fast.

The computation results can be clearly seen that population size affects the operation time greatly. Whether the program runs on the CPU platform or GPU platform, the time-consumption will increase with population size increasing, but the acceleration effect becomes much more significant after being paralleled. Figure 8 shows the speedup ratio of CPU-GPU Heterogeneous Model. It indicates that when the population size is 1000, the simulation is accelerated at 9× after being paralleled. When the population size rises to 5000, the simulation is accelerated at 20× speed. Therefore, the CPU-GPU model in this paper has high operating efficiency.

This experimental result reflects the acceleration trend of the parallel program because the random search technique is used in NSGA II. The trend indicates that the average running time and speedup ratio of CPU-GPU heterogeneous model are productive.

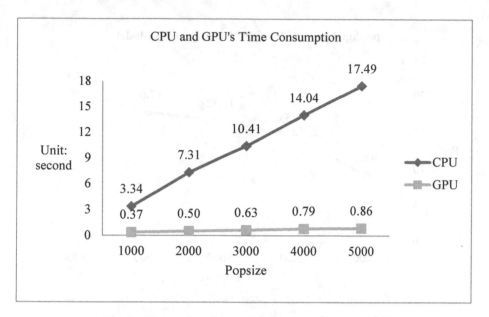

**Fig. 6.** The average time consumption of CPU and GPU

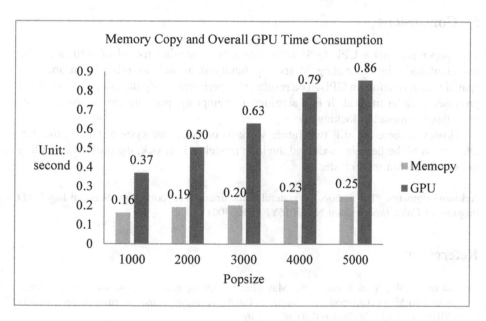

**Fig. 7.** Memory copy and overall GPU time consumption

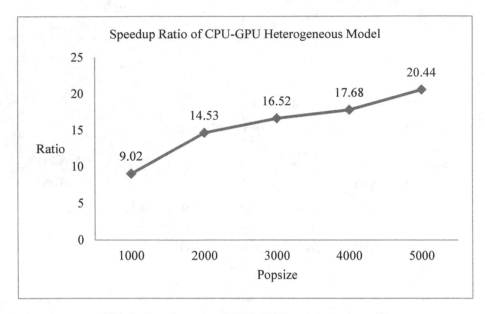

**Fig. 8.** Speedup ratio of CPU-GPU heterogeneous model

## 5  Conclusions

This paper presents a CPU-GPU heterogeneous computing model of iFitDock. The model offloads the computing of scoring functions as well as related conformation spatial transformation on GPU. The results of experiment verify the effectiveness of the proposed parallel method. It is a significant attempt to speed up the performance of semi-flexible modular docking.

However, there are still two future work to enhance our system. One is the parallelization of the flexible mode and the loop model of iFitDock, the other is extending the system to run on a cluster.

**Acknowledgments.** The authors are grateful to the financial supports from National Key R&D Program of China (under Grant No. 2016YFA0502300).

## References

1. Ritchie, D.W., Venkatraman, V., Mavridis, L.: Using graphics processors to accelerate protein docking calculations. In: Studies in Health Technology and Informatics, pp. 146–155 (2010). doi:10.3233/978-1-60750-583-9-146
2. Moustakas, D.T., Lang, P.T., Pegg, S., Pettersen, E., Kuntz, I.D., Brooijmans, N., Rizzo, R. C.: Development and validation of a modular, extensible docking program: DOCK 5. J. Comput.-Aided Mol. Des. **20**, 601–619 (2006). doi:10.1007/s10822-006-9060-4
3. Wu, J., Chen, C., Hong, B.: A GPU-based approach to accelerate computational protein-DNA docking. Comput. Sci. Eng. **14**, 20–29 (2012). doi:10.1186/1477-5956-10-S1-S17

4. Korb, O., Stützle, T., Exner, T.E.: Accelerating molecular docking calculations using graphics processing units. J. Chem. Inf. Model. **51**, 865–876 (2011). doi:10.1021/ci100459b

5. Anthopoulos, A., Pasqualetto, G., Grimstead, I., Brancale, A.: Haptic-driven, interactive drug design: implementing a GPU-based approach to evaluate the induced fit effect. Faraday Discuss. **169**, 323–342 (2014). doi:10.1039/c3fd00139c

6. Yang, H., Li, B., Wang, Y., Luan, Z., Qian, D., Chu, T.: Accelerating Dock6's amber scoring with graphic processing unit. In: Hsu, C.-H., Yang, L.T., Park, J.H., Yeo, S.-S. (eds.) ICA3PP 2010. LNCS, vol. 6081, pp. 404–415. Springer, Heidelberg (2010). doi:10.1007/978-3-642-13119-6_35

7. Altuntaş, S., Bozkus, Z., Fraguela, B.B.: GPU accelerated molecular docking simulation with genetic algor ithms. In: Squillero, G., Burelli, P. (eds.) EvoApplications 2016. LNCS, vol. 9598, pp. 134–146. Springer, Cham (2016). doi:10.1007/978-3-319-31153-1_10

8. Sukhwani, B., Herbordt, M.C.: FPGA acceleration of rigid-molecule docking codes. IET Comput. Digital Tech. **4**, 184–195 (2010). doi:10.1049/iet-cdt.2009.0013

9. Bai, F., Xu, Y., Chen, J., Liu, Q., Gu, J., Wang, X., Ma, J., Li, H., Onuchic, J.N., Jiang, H.: Free energy landscape for the binding process of Huperzine A to acetylcholinesterase. Proc. Nat. Acad. Sci. U.S.A. **110**, 4273–4278 (2013). doi:10.1073/pnas.1301814110

10. Deb, K., Pratap, A., Agarwal, S., Meyarivan, T.: A fast and elitist multiobjective genetic algorithm: NSGA-II. IEEE Trans. Evol. Comput. **6**, 182–197 (2002). doi:10.1109/4235.996017

# FixCaffe: Training CNN with Low Precision Arithmetic Operations by Fixed Point Caffe

Shasha Guo, Lei Wang$^{(\boxtimes)}$, Baozi Chen, Qiang Dou, Yuxing Tang, and Zhisheng Li

College of Computer, National University of Defense and Technology, Changsha, Hunan, China
leiwang@nudt.edu.cn

**Abstract.** The convolutional neural networks are widely used in deep learning model because of its advantages in image classification, speech recognition and natural language processing. However, training large-scale networks is very time and resource consuming, because it is both compute-intensive and memory-intensive. In this paper, we proposed to use the fixed point arithmetic to train CNN with popular deep learning framework Caffe. We propose our framework FixCaffe (Fixed Point Caffe), where fixed point matrix multiply function is substitute for part of the original floating point matrix multiply function in Caffe. We analyze the range of the operands during the training process, and choose the proper scaling factor for transform floating point operands to fixed point operands. Training LeNet-S model, obtained by modifying LeNet-5, on the MNIST benchmark, the result shows that after training 1000 iterations, FixCaffe with 8-bit fixed point multiplications only leads to about 0.5% loss in the classification accuracy compared to the single-precision floating point Caffe baseline. Using Xilinx V7 690T to implement the multiplier, the cost of computing resource can save up to 83.3%, and the on-chip storage overhead for the LeNet-S model's parameters can save 75%.

**Keywords:** CNN · Limited precision · CNN training · Accuracy · Caffe

## 1 Introduction

Deep learning have demonstrated state-of-the-art performance in many machine learning tasks such as image classification, speech recognition and natural language processing. One of the most impressive forms of deep learning architecture is Convolutional Neural Network (CNN). CNNs are primarily used to solve challenging image classification tasks, avoiding the complex pre-processing of images.

Since AlexNet won the 2012 ImageNet large-scale image recognition competition (ILSVRC2012) with 83.6% top-5 accuracy [11], CNNs have become well known. In 2014, VGGNet [16] achieves 92.7% top-5 accuracy on ImageNet and

© Springer International Publishing AG 2017
Y. Dou et al. (Eds.): APPT 2017, LNCS 10561, pp. 38–50, 2017.
DOI: 10.1007/978-3-319-67952-5_4

in the same year GoogLeNet [17] achieves 93.3%. By 2015, Microsoft's residual learning framework, ResNet [9], achieves 96.43% top-5 accuracy, exceeding human accuracy which is only 94.9%. These networks are very deep especially the last one which is more than 100 layers.

To a large extent, the success of deep learning architecture is contingent upon the underlying hardware platform ability to perform fast, supervised training of complex networks using large amount of labeled data. Virtually all training today is in floating point [10], which needs massive computation power and storage requirements, and *Graphics Processing Unit* (GPU) provides enough computing to develop them. Therefore, training is often executed in the data-centers with GPUs deployed. Recently, Google design a new hardware called a *Tensor Processing Unit* (TPU) which can use only 8-bit for inference [10], and the latest TPU2 can perform both training and inference in low-precision data representation and fixed point arithmetic.

There are two main motivations to adopt low numerical precision by using fixed point representation at training. Firstly, fixed point computation units are typically faster and use far less hardware resources and power than floating point computation units. The smaller logic footprint of the fixed point arithmetic circuits would allow for the instantiation of many more such units for a given area and power budget. Secondly, low-precision data representation reduces the memory footprint, enabling larger models to fit within the given memory capacity and lowering the bandwidth requirements [6].

In order to reduce computation and storage resources consumption in the hardware implementation, this paper implemented a framework FixCaffe to train CNN using low-precision fixed point arithmetic based on the deep learning framework Caffe. The main contributions are,

- By analyzing the effect of converting single-precision floating point operations of different CNN layers into low-precision fixed point computations, we determine which operation can be converted and which one cannot.
- We propose a method of converting floating point numbers into fixed point integers for data in CNN training. The method includes analyzing data distribution, choosing scaling-up method and deciding the rounding scheme.
- By modifying the deep learning framework Caffe, we implement a framework called FixCaffe to support low-precision fixed point matrix multiplication.

With the experiment of LeNet-S, it shows that after training 1000 iterations, FixCaffe with 8-bit precision multiplications only lead to about 0.5% loss in the classification accuracy compared to the single precision floating point baseline. Using implementation on Xilinx V7 690T FPGA, the cost of computing resource can save up to 83.3%, and the on-chip storage overhead for the LeNet-S model's parameters can save 75%.

# 2    Background

## 2.1    LeNet-5

LeNet-5 [12] is a classical CNN model for image recognition. Our model, LeNet-S, is obtained by modifying LeNet-5. As can be seen from Fig. 1, LeNet-S comprises of 9 layers. Specific parameters of each layer except data layer are shown in Table 1.

The convolutional (CONV) layer is to detect the local connection characteristics of the previous layer. The units of a CONV layer is organized by feature maps. Each feature map has many neurons, each connected to a local region of the input feature map through a set of weights. All neurons of the same feature map share the same set of weights, also called the convolutional kernel. Different feature maps use different filter banks. In conclusion, each feature map extracts a feature of the input via a convolutional kernel. The pooling layer fuses semantic-similar features into a single one. A typical pooling layer, max pooling layer, computes the local maximum for each feature map/several feature maps. The fully connected (FC) layer plays an important role in classification in CNN, mapping the learned features to the sample label space. Non-linear layer is to perform non-linear transformation for input data and produce output as same size as input.

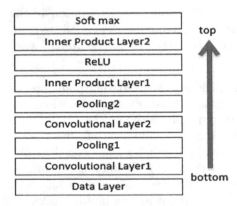

**Table 1.** Parameters of LeNet-S model

| Layer type | Weight | Bias |
|---|---|---|
| Data layer | | |
| Conv1 | $20 * 1 * 5 * 5$ | 20 |
| Pooling1 | | |
| Conv2 | $50 * 20 * 5 * 5$ | 50 |
| Pooling2 | | |
| Ip1 | $800 * 500$ | 500 |
| ReLU | | |
| Ip2 | $500 * 10$ | 10 |
| Soft max | | |

**Fig. 1.** LeNet-S model structure

## 2.2    CNN Training and Caffe Implementation

The training of CNN includes two process: forward and backward propagation.

**Forward.** In the forward propagation phase, the data source is from the data read layer and passes through several processing layers to the last layer (possibly the loss layer or the feature extraction layer). Weights in the network do not change during the forward propagation phase and can be considered as constants. The calculation can be expressed as a formula:

$$a_i^{(l)} = \sum_j w_{i,j}^{(l)} \cdot g\left(a_j^{(l-1)}\right). \tag{1}$$

where $a_i^{(l)}$ denotes the i-th activation in the l-th layer, $w_{i,j}^{(l)}$ represents the (i, j)-th weight value in the l-th layer. And $g(\cdot)$ is the activation function.

**Backward.** Backward propagation computes the gradient of each parameter in the network from top to bottom by loss function. All the weight layers update parameters with these gradient together after one backward propagation. The loss function is the starting point of the backward propagation and is obtained in the forward propagation calculation. And the purpose of backward is to minimize the loss function.

Backward is a process of matrix operations as well as forward.

**Main Computation in CNN Training in Caffe.** In this paper, we aim to modify the popular deep learning framework, Caffe, to train CNN with fixed point arithmetics. Thus we will introduce some details of Caffe and find the main computations in CNN training in Caffe.

There are three important data structure used in Caffe, *Net*, *Layer* and *Blob*. *Net* includes both *Layer* objects and *Blob* objects. *Blob* is used to *Layer* data, such as weights, biases, inputs, outputs and gradients. Layer performs some computations on the specific input *Blob* based on the *Net* description, and produces output *Blob* [18].

Caffe requires Basic Linear Algebra Subprograms (BLAS) as the backend of its matrix and vector computations, which are the main mathematical calculations in CNN training. There are several implementations of this library, such as ATLAS, Inter MKL, OpenBLAS and so on. In this paper, we use OpenBLAS. Two functions, *gemm()* and *gemv()*, are commonly used. The former is basic matrix-matrix multiplication (MM) routine, and the latter is basic matrix-vector product operation.

Two specific layer types, CONV layer and FC layer, are worth considering. The former contributes to the majority (e.g., 86.5–97.8%) of the total computing time and the latter contributes to more than 87.1% of the total memory storage cost of the model [15]. As a result, these two layer types have significant influence on the cost of computing and storage resources. MM operations are the main computing type in these two layer types. For convolutional layers, Caffe use *im2col* method to convert input and kernel into two matrices and substitute MM operation for convolution process in the forward propagation, while in backward computation of gradients is achieved by computing the partial derivatives of input, weights and biases, which, except biases, are MM operations. For fully connected layers, as Caffe adopts batch processing, input vectors composes the input matrix and it multiply with the weight matrix to produce output in forward, and in backward the calculations are similar to those in the convolutional layer. Therefore, we conclude that in Caffe, MM operation is the main computation in CNN training.

## 3   Overview of FixCaffe

Figure 2 gives the main idea of FixCaffe. Since MM operation is the main computation in Caffe's training CNN, converting MM operation from single-precision floating point arithmetic to limited-precision fixed point is the key point of implementing FixCaffe. We propose a method to transform operands of MM operation from single-precision floating point to limited-precision fixed point. First, we amplify data with scaling factors to get integer part of the amplified data, and then apply the rounding scheme to limit the value of the fixed point integer within the range of a low numerical precision. Scaling factors are numbers. Their value are of significance to the training performance. To select proper scaling factors, we use Caffe to train CNN on the given dataset for a few iterations with single-precision floating point arithmetic, profiling weights and intermediate data (such as inputs, outputs and gradients). By analyzing data distribution, we choose candidate scaling factors. Next, we compute error between MM operation outputs of original Caffe (OpenBLAS-based) and FixCaffe and determine scaling factors based on error distribution. The limited-precision fixed point data will be the input of fixed point MM operation. Using limited-precision fixed point MM operation to replace original single-precision floating point MM operation in weight layers' forward and backward propagation in Caffe, we get FixCaffe. At last, we use FixCaffe to train CNN on the given dataset to get an available model for feeding to hardware inference engine.

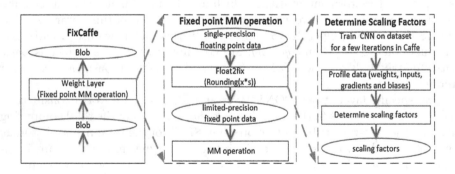

**Fig. 2.** Overview of FixCaffe

MM operation is exactly a multiply-and-accumulate process, just as Eq. 1 shows. Assuming that in Eq. 1 $w$ and $g(a)$ (operands of MM operation) are $a$-bit fixed point values, the computing process can be divided into the following two steps.

Step 1: Compute $w \cdot g(a)$. As both $w$ and $g(a)$ are $a$-bit fixed point values, the product is a $2a$-bit value.

Step 2: Compute $\sum w \cdot g(a)$. The size of the accumulator is larger than $2a$-bit to prevent overflow.

In this paper we use low precision multiplication but high precision accumulation to prevent overflow.

The outcome of equation $a_i^{(l)}$ in next layer is equivalent to $a_j^{(l-1)}$ in this layer. To keep with the desired fixed point precision, we add a quantization step. We divide the outcome by $w$'s scaling factor and this is conducted on CPU rather than hardware.

## 3.1 Float2fix

**Rounding Scheme.** To convert data from floating point into limited-precision fixed point, we first scale up the number by a scaling factor which can be denoted as $s$ and take the integer part of the amplified floating point number. The equation is:

$$y = \lfloor x \times s \rfloor. \tag{2}$$

Then use rounding scheme to limit the integer part of the number in the range of given precision, which can be described as follows:

$$Round(y) = \begin{cases} -2^{FL}, & y < -2^{FL}, \\ y, & -2^{FL} \leqslant y \leqslant 2^{FL} - 1, \\ 2^{FL} - 1, & y > 2^{FL} - 1. \end{cases} \tag{3}$$

**Scaling Factor.** Scaling factor is crucial to the computing error between result of limited-precision fixed point multiplication and traditional single-precision floating point. The influence comes from two aspects with relation to Eqs. 2 and 3. In Eq. 2, it will lead to the loss of data distribution information if the scaling factor is too small because the integer part of the amplified number is 0. In Eq. 3, it will lead to the loss of data distribution information if the scaling factor is too big because the integer is out of range and will be rounded.

We give the norm and procedure to choose proper scaling factors for training.

*Norm.*

$$Error = \frac{\frac{\sum_{i=0}^{M \times N} |C[i] - D[i]|}{M \times N}}{\frac{\sum_{i=0}^{M \times N} |C[i]|}{M \times N}} = \frac{\sum_{i=0}^{M \times N} |C[i] - D[i]|}{\sum_{i=0}^{M \times N} |C[i]|} \tag{4}$$

In 4, C represents the result of MM operation in single-precision floating point format, D is the result of MM operation in limited-precision fixed point format, and $M \times N$ is the size of C and D.

Scaling factors leading to small *Error* are more likely to make training converge than those leading to big *Error*.

*Procedure.* The procedure can be divided into three steps.

(1) Train the model in floating point using the target data set and collect statistics of operands of MM operations, such as weights and inputs for each weight layer in the early several iterations.
(2) Analyze the data distribution and select candidate scaling factors for each kind of operands of MM operations.
(3) Compute error and determine the best scaling factors for different data precision from the candidates.

# 4   Implementation and Experimental Result

## 4.1   Platform

We use MNIST dataset as the benchmark. This dataset comprises of 60,000 training images and 10,000 test images. Each image is 28 × 28 pixels containing a digit from 0 to 9. The FixCaffe framework is running on Ubuntu 16.04 system in VMware 12.0 Workstation. The processor is Intel Core i5-6600.

## 4.2   Implementation

We use Eigen as the alternative library of OpenBLAS to support fixed point operations in Caffe because OpenBLAS only supports floating point operations. Eigen doesn't have any dependencies other than the C++ standard library [1], and provides fixed point matrix operations which are equivalent to *gemm/gemv* in OpenBLAS [2]. Note that matrix reading from memory is RowMajor in BLAS but ColMajor in Eigen by default. We use our function, eigen_gemm to replace the call of *gemm* in CONV and FC layers' forward and backward propagation as shown in Table 2.

**Table 2.** Functions calling *gemm*

| Functions | Phase |
| --- | --- |
| forward_cpu_gemm | Forward |
| forward_cpu_bias | Forward |
| backward_cpu_gemm | Backward |
| weight_cpu_gemm | Backward |

## 4.3   Choosing Scaling Factors for Training LeNet-S with MNIST

**Analyzing Data Distribution and Choosing Candidates.** Table 3 gives the operands of MM operations during the forward and backward propagation of the four weight layers of LeNet-S model.

**Table 3.** Operands of MM operations

|   | Operand1 | Operand2 |
|---|----------|----------|
| 1 | bottom_data | weight |
| 2 | bias | bias_multiplier_ |
| 3 | top_diff | bottom_data |
| 4 | top_diff | weight |

**Table 4.** Candidate scaling factors

|   | s1 | s2 |
|---|----|----|
| bottom_data | 10 | 100 |
| weight | 100 | 1000 |
| top_diff | 1000 | 10000 |
| bias | 100 | |

Table 3 shows that there are total five kinds of operands, of which all elements of matrix bias_multiplier_ are number 1 in LeNet-S model. Therefore, we only analyze data distribution of the other four operand types. Data samples are fetched from MM operations of weight layers during training LeNet-S on MNIST for a few iterations using floating point arithmetic. Figure 3 gives the results.

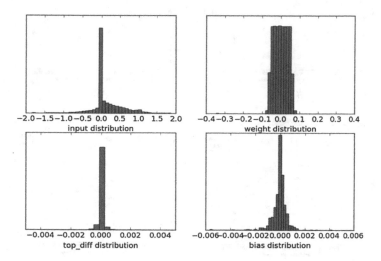

**Fig. 3.** Data distribution

From Fig. 3 we can see that most of the input data is between −0.1 and 0.1, so are the weights. Data of top_diff is very small and the majority is below 0.001. Based on the results above, we choose two candidate scaling factors for bottom_data, weight and top_diff, as shown in Table 4. Because the amount of biases is very small, accounting for a little of the total computations and memory cost, we choose 100 as the final scaling factor based on Fig. 3.

**Calculating Error.** Figure 4 gives error distribution of MM operations in Table 3 (except for bias and bias_multiplier_) when using different candidate scaling factors for converting the floating point operands into limited-precision fixed point format. Data samples come from early 20 iterations of training LeNet-S model with MNIST using floating point arithmetic.

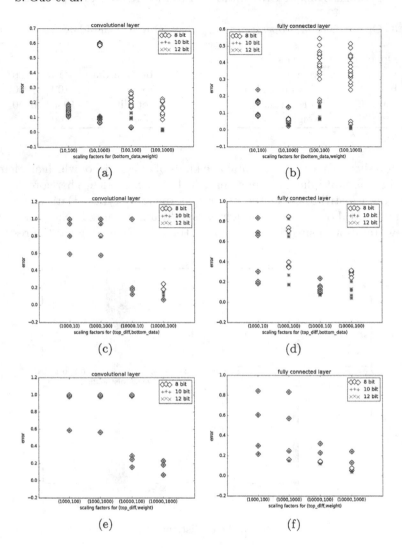

**Fig. 4.** Error distribution

In Fig. 4, the x axis is scaling factors for MM operation's two operands and the y axis is *Error*. From Fig. 4 we can see that data points in 10-bit and 12-bit precision are the same, which means 10-bit is sufficient for representing the amplified integer. Therefore, we do not conduct experiments in 12-bit.

Take 8-bit as an example, from Fig. 4(a) and (b) we find that *Error* is smallest when scaling factors for bottom_data and weight are 10 and 100 respectively. Figure 4(c) to (f) show that error is smaller if top_diff is 10000 rather than 1000 when scaling factors of bottom_data and weight are 10 and 100. Similarly, we determine scaling factors under 10-bit. Table 5 shows our decision.

**Table 5.** Scaling factors for MM operation operands under different data precision

| Precision | $s$ for bottom_data | $s$ for weight | $s$ for top_diff | $s$ for bias |
|-----------|--------------------|----------------|------------------|--------------|
| 8         | 10                 | 100            | 10000            | 100          |
| 10        | 100                | 1000           | 10000            | 100          |

## 4.4   Comparison of Classification Accuracy

We use the conventional 32-bit floating point representation as our baseline, where matrix operation functions called by layer forward and backward propagation are also implemented by Eigen.

While training using fixed point, the different model hyper-parameters such as weight initialization, regularization parameters, learning rates etc. are kept unchanged from the ones used during the baseline evaluation.

For each configuration of training, we train 6 times, 3 with max iterations of 1000 and the others with max iterations of 5000 to observe the performance (the accuracy on the test net).

Figure 5 shows the comparison of classification accuracy between baseline and experimental group as shown in Table 5 using FixCaffe.

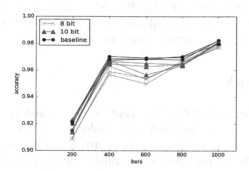

**Fig. 5.** Accuracy comparison

From Fig. 5 we can see that with 10-bit data precision limit, training with fixed point MM operation leads to nearly no loss in accuracy after 1000 iterations. And 8-bit causes only about 0.3% decline in accuracy after 1000 iterations.

## 4.5   Discussion

**Cost of Computing Resource.** The cost of a fixed point multiplier varies as the square of the precision (of its operands) for small widths while the cost of adders and accumulators varies as a linear function of the precision [5]. As a result, the cost of a fixed point multiplier-accumulator mainly depends on the precision of the multiplier. In modern FPGAs, multipliers can be implemented with dedicated DSP blocks/slices. One Xilinx V7 690T has 3600 DSP blocks. We use $n_x$ to denote the number of x-bit wide multipliers one Xilinx V7 690T can implement, and $N$ to denote the number of total multipliers the digital implementation of LeNet-S model needs. One DSP block/slice can implement one $27 \times 27$ multiplier, two $18 \times 18$ multipliers or three $9 \times 9$ multipliers. The ratio of computing cost is:

$$\frac{cost_a}{cost_b} = \frac{\frac{N}{n_a}}{\frac{N}{n_b}} = \frac{n_b}{n_a}, \tag{5}$$

where $a$ means a-bit and $b$ means b-bit. A $32 \times 32$ multiplier needs two DSP block. So $n_{32}$ is 1800, $n_{10}$ is 7200 and $n_8$ is 10800. Therefore, implementing 8-bit wide multiplier compared to 32-bit wide multiplier can save $1 - \frac{n_{32}}{n_8} = 1 - \frac{1800}{10800} = 83.3\%$ computing resources.

**Cost of Memory Footprint.** Take LeNet-S as an example. From Table 1 we know the total number of weights in LeNet-S is 430500, and that of bias is 580, and the sum is 431080. Biases account for only about 0.001%. With a single-precision floating point representation, these weights require $431080 * 4 = 1724320$ bytes of storage space. The 10-bit fixed point (the most significant is sign bit) can represent $(-2048, 2047)$. Only 31.25% of the original storage space. The 8-bit fixed point (the most significant is sign bit) can represent $(-128, 127)$, requiring only 25% of the original storage space.

## 5    Related Work

Determining the precision of the data representation and the compute units is a critical design choice in the hardware (analog or digital) implementation of artificial neural networks. In general, there are two approaches to designing a fixed point DCN [13]: (1) convert a pre-trained floating point DCN model into a fixed point model without training, and (2) train a DCN model with fixed point constraint.

There are several works related to the first approach. One of them is to fine-tune pre-trained floating point DCNs using data representations with reduced numeric precision. However, the training algorithms have a strong tendency to diverge when the precision of network parameters and features are too low [3,8].

More recently, several works have touched upon the second approach, training deep networks with low numerical precision [6,7,14]. In all of these works, stochastic rounding has been the key to improving the convergence properties of the training algorithm. Stochastic rounding is an unbiased rounding scheme and possesses the desirable property that the expected rounding error is zero [6]. And another work is also worth mentioning. In [4], they propose that using dynamic fixed point is even better than fixed point. The dynamic fixed point format is a variant of the fixed point format in which there are several scaling factors instead of a single one. It can be seen as a compromise between the floating point format and the fixed point format. With dynamic fixed point, a few grouped variables share a scaling factor which is updated from time to time to reflect the statistics of values in the group [4].

Our work is training CNN with limited-precision data representation and fixed point multiply operation.

## 6   Conclusion

This paper explore the effect of using limited precision data representation and computation on training of convolutional neural networks. We substitute the Matrix Multiply Library of Caffe from OpenBLAS to Eigen, and use LeNet-S model as an training example. We find that it is acceptable to use low-precision fixed point data representation and multiplication for training LeNet-S with MNIST datset. The experimental result shows that after training 1000 iterations, FixCaffe using 8-bit fixed point multiplications only leads to about 0.5% loss in the classification accuracy compared to the single-precision floating point Caffe baseline. Using Xilinx V7 690T to implement the multiplier, the cost of computing resource can save up to 83.3%, and the on-chip storage overhead for the LeNet-S model's parameters can save 75%. The future work is to explore whether low precision computation works for networks deeper than LeNet-S.

**Acknowlegement.** Funding provided by China NSFC 61402501, 61602498. Thanks to the anonymous reviewers.

## References

1. http://eigen.tuxfamily.org/index.php?title=Main_Page
2. https://eigen.tuxfamily.org/dox-devel/TopicUsingBlasLapack.html
3. Courbariaux, M., Bengio, Y., David, J.P.: Low precision arithmetic for deep learning. Eprint Arxiv (2014)
4. Courbariaux, M., Bengio, Y., David, J.P.: Training deep neural networks with low precision multiplications. Computer Science (2014)
5. David, J.P., Kalach, K., Tittley, N.: Hardware complexity of modular multiplication and exponentiation. IEEE Trans. Comput. **56**(10), 1308–1319 (2007)
6. Gupta, S., Agrawal, A., Gopalakrishnan, K., Narayanan, P.: Deep learning with limited numerical precision. Computer Science (2015)
7. Gysel, P., Motamedi, M., Ghiasi, S.: Hardware-oriented approximation of convolutional neural networks (2016)
8. Han, S., Mao, H., Dally, W.J.: A deep neural network compression pipeline: pruning, quantization, huffman encoding (2015)
9. He, K., Zhang, X., Ren, S., Sun, J.: Deep residual learning for image recognition. In: Computer Vision and Pattern Recognition, pp. 770–778 (2016)
10. Jouppi, N.P., Young, C., Patil, N., Patterson, D., Agrawal, G., Bajwa, R., Bates, S., Bhatia, S., Boden, N., Borchers, A.: In-datacenter performance analysis of a tensor processing unit (2017)

11. Krizhevsky, A., Sutskever, I., Hinton, G.E.: Imagenet classification with deep convolutional neural networks. In: International Conference on Neural Information Processing Systems, pp. 1097–1105 (2012)
12. Lecun, Y., Bottou, L., Bengio, Y., Haffner, P.: Gradient-based learning applied to document recognition. Proc. IEEE **86**(11), 2278–2324 (1998)
13. Lin, D.D., Talathi, S.S., Sreekanth Annapureddy, V.: Fixed point quantization of deep convolutional networks. Computer Science (2016)
14. Lin, Z., Courbariaux, M., Memisevic, R., Bengio, Y.: Neural networks with few multiplications (2016)
15. Mao, J., Chen, X., Nixon, K.W., Krieger, C., Chen, Y.: MoDNN: local distributed mobile computing system for deep neural network. In: Design, Automation Test in Europe Conference Exhibition (DATE), pp. 1396–1401, March 2017
16. Simonyan, K., Zisserman, A.: Very deep convolutional networks for large-scale image recognition. Computer Science (2014)
17. Szegedy, C., Liu, W., Jia, Y., Sermanet, P., Reed, S., Anguelov, D., Erhan, D., Vanhoucke, V., Rabinovich, A.: Going deeper with convolutions, pp. 1–9 (2014)
18. Zhao, Y.: Deep Learning: Learn Caffe in 21 Days (2016)

# SysMon: Monitoring Memory Behaviors via OS Approach

Mengyao Xie[1,2,3], Lei Liu[1,2(✉)], Hao Yang[1,2,3], Chenggang Wu[2], and Hongna Geng[1,2,3]

[1] Sys-Inventor Research Group, Beijing, China
[2] State Key Laboratory of Computer Architecture, ICT, CAS, Beijing, China
[3] University of Chinese Academy of Sciences, Beijing, China
{xiemengyao,liulei2010}@ict.ac.cn

**Abstract.** To capture and analyze applications' memory behaviors with low overhead plays a vital role in managing and scheduling memory resources on modern computer systems. In this paper, we re-design SysMon based on [13, 14], which is an OS-level memory behaviors monitoring module in existing OS, and modify its several core components to meet the challenges of higher efficiency and accuracy. SysMon can be used without offline profiling, instrumentation or configuring complex parameters. We evaluate SysMon by making a great deal of experiments on SPECCPU 2006 [7], Memcached [1] and Redis [6]. The experimental results show that, by using SysMon, we can efficiently capture the memory footprint, write/read operations, hot/cold features, re-use time, bank hotness/bank balance, etc. Besides, we collect the memory access behaviors in the configuration of different sampling intervals, and draw a conclusion that using a 3 s interval can obtain information accurately with low overhead. Finally, to reduce the scanning overhead during samplings, SysMon adopts a randomization method, and scans only a portion of pages. Experiments show that the sampling overhead can be reduced by 44.42% on average while guaranteeing the accuracy of sampling.

**Keywords:** Memory behaviors · System monitor tool · Random sampling · Sampling interval

## 1 Introduction

Allocating, managing and scheduling of memory resources have always been a major and very challenging subject on modern computer systems. With the emerging of big data and cloud computing, fast-growing memory footprint and energy consumption, high demand for Quality of Service (QoS) and throughput, etc. have brought new challenges to memory management [20–23, 25]. Especially, it may result in the severer memory access conflict with high probability when multiple applications are running in parallel. Many previous studies [8, 9, 13, 16, 19, 26, 27] show that it is important for

This work is supported by NSF of China under grants No. 61502452 (PI: Lei Liu).

© Springer International Publishing AG 2017
Y. Dou et al. (Eds.): APPT 2017, LNCS 10561, pp. 51–63, 2017.
DOI: 10.1007/978-3-319-67952-5_5

operating systems to efficiently manage data with low overhead. In order to achieve this goal, there are many factors need to be considered to manage memory system efficiently, such as the different characteristics of data (e.g., write/read operations, hot/cold features), memory access hotness, re-use time, etc. Thus, an effective memory management policy is expected to accurately detect the applications' memory behaviors and schedule memory resources accordingly.

The existing program analysis tools like Intel's dynamic binary instrumentation framework Pin [5] can be used to create Pintools to perform program analysis on user space applications on Linux, Windows and OS X*. However, instrumentation consumes system resources, and thus increases the profiling overhead when analyzing the applications' behaviors. Another tool, Oprofile [2], is a performance counter monitor tool that monitors the running applications based on Performance Monitoring Unit (PMU). However, Oprofile and other performance counter monitor tools like PAPI [3] and perfmon2 [4] require underlying hardware support (i.e., PMU). And many of them cannot fully support the newer architectures because of the diversification of the hardware architecture.

Compared with above approaches, SysMon [13, 14] is an efficient and lightweight application access behaviors monitor tool, which is a module that integrated into the kernel. It can be used on any version of Linux kernel without instrumentation, configuring complex parameters, or extra underlying hardware support. SysMon has good compatibility, stability, and scalability. However, in practice, some studies further show that the overhead brought by SysMon is heavy for some applications with much higher memory footprint and the sampling interval is hard to be determined to balance the overhead and accuracy in many real cases. To address these concerns, we re-design SysMon and make the following contributions in this paper:

- We optimize SysMon's sample method by adopting random sampling rather than traversing the page table to sample each page. The experimental results show that the sampling overhead can reduce 44.42% on average while ensuring the sample effect.
- We collect the memory access information under the configuration of different sampling intervals. By analyzing the information, we draw a conclusion that using a 3 s interval can obtain information accurately with low overhead.
- By using SysMon, we study a large number of workloads, and analyze their characteristics, including SPECCPU2006 [7], Memcached [1] and Redis [6].

We open sourced SysMon. The full code of SysMon is available at: https://github.com/Sys-Inventor-Research-Group-ICT/Sysmon.

## 2　Background

### 2.1　__access_bit and __dirty_bit

Starting from Linux v2.6.11, 64-bit Operating System (OS) adopts the organizational form of the four-layer page table, which is represented in Fig. 1. Each item in Page Global Directory (PGD) points to a Page Upper Directory (PUD), and each entry in PUD points to a Page Middle Directory (PMD), and then, each item in PMD points to a PTE.

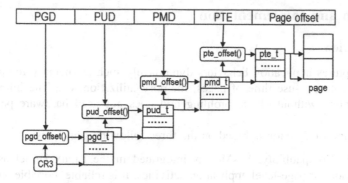

**Fig. 1.** Four-layer page table under 64-bit operating system.

The *__access_bit* in page table entry (PTE) can be used to indicate whether the page is accessed [11, 18]. 0 represents the page has not been accessed; while 1 means accessed (we define these pages as hot pages in this paper). And for the *__dirty_bit*, it can represent whether the page is modified. Similar to the *__access_bit*, when the *__dirty_bit* is equal to 0, it means there is no write operation happened to that page.

## 2.2 Address Mapping

Prior research [28] shows that mainstream computer systems' address mapping can be detected by the software method. For example, as shown in Fig. 2, bank bits are divided into two parts. Part I is independent, and part II is overlapped with cache bits. Figure 2(a) presents Intel i7-860 processor that equips with a 16-way set associative 8 MB last level cache (LLC) and 8 GB DDR3 main memory system, and it's bank bits are 13–15, 21 and 22 bits; In Fig. 2(b), Intel Xeon 5600 processor, with 16-way set associative 12 MB LLC and 32 GB DDR3 main memory, whose bank bits are 13, 14, 20 and 21 bits. For the configuration (a), 5 bank bits can index $2^5 = 32$ banks ranging from bank 0 to bank 31.

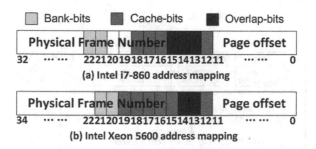

**Fig. 2.** Address mapping.

# 3 Design and Implementation

## 3.1 Overview

SysMon captures application behaviors dynamically such as memory footprint, page access frequency, re-use time of pages, memory utilization, etc. The information is collected online without offline profiling and does not need hardware performance counters.

The design of SysMon is based on the three following principles:

**Principle 1:** Compatibility. SysMon is integrated in the Linux kernel as a kernel module to monitor page-level application activities. It is reliable, portable and suitable for any version of Linux kernel.

**Principle 2:** Low overhead. SysMon is a lightweight online tool that monitors applications in the real time. The overhead is mainly caused by scanning application's page table. Through the random scanning optimization method, which is introduced in detail at Chapter 5, SysMon greatly reduces the scanning overhead by 44.42% on average.

**Principle 3:** Efficiency. It is important for a monitoring tool that does not slow the responses to the applications' access requests. Our experiments show that 100 μs is enough to collect sufficient information while incurring a negligible delay.

Except for monitoring the single application, SysMon can also monitor multiple applications that are executed in parallel. By analyzing the information captured by SysMon, we can make an accurate prediction of a running workload's memory characteristics, and use an appropriate memory management policy.

As shown in Fig. 3, we take a page classification algorithm as an example to introduce the modules of SysMon. The information in the dashed box is collected by SysMon, and *acc_num* records the page's total number of accesses in a given period, *read/write times* are being used to indicate the number of read/write operations on the pages during samplings. *Re-use time* is a variable to represent the page's temporal locality. Based on the information in the dashed box in Fig. 3, we classify the pages into three categories: write page, read page and cold page. In our experiments, *THR1* is 20

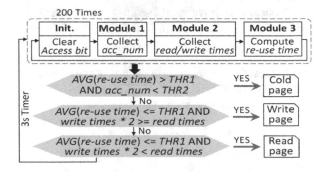

**Fig. 3.** SysMon-based online page classification algorithm.

and *THR2* is 10. The detailed information about pages' characteristics can guide the data placement and data movement among the DRAM Banks to improve the overall performance.

In the next section, we will introduce the modules of SysMon one by one.

## 3.2 Module 1: Collecting Page Access Frequency

In the current version, the time interval between two sampling periods is 3 s in our system. To reduce the error efficiently, 200 samplings are executed in one sampling period (i.e., 3 s), but note that the time cost of 200 samplings is far less than 3 s (100 ns in most cases). Each sampling contains two loops. Firstly, SysMon clears pages' *__access_bit* by the *pte_mkold()* kernel function; and secondly, SysMon checks the pages' *__access_bit* in the second loop. If the *__access_bit* is still 0, it means the page has not been accessed in this sampling; otherwise, this page has been accessed during this sampling.

---

**Algorithm_1:** Calculate Access Frequency and Write / Read Times of Pages
**Output:** (1) hot_page [ ]; (2) write_times [ ]; (3) read_times [ ]

---

1. **FOR** i **FROM** 0 **TO** ITERATIONS **DO** // default 200
2.    Clear __access_bit, __dirty_bit of all pages;
3.    **FOR** each page P **IN** an application **DO**
4.        Obtain PTE of page P via P's address;
5.        **IF** pte_present (PTE) **THEN**    // P is in the memory
6.            **IF** pte_young (PTE) **THEN**    // P has been accessed
7.                hot_page [P] ← hot_page [P]; // access frequency
8.                **IF** ( pte_dirty (PTE) ) **THEN**    // write operation
9.                    write_times [P] ← write_times [P] + 1;
10.               **ELSE**  // read operation
11.                   read_times [P] ← read_times [P] + 1;
12.               **END IF**
13.           **END IF**
14.       **END IF**
15.   **END FOR**
16. **END FOR**
17. **RETURN** hot_page [ ], write_times [ ], read_times [ ];

\* hot_page [ ] is an array representing access frequency of each page.
\* write_times [ ] is an array that records write times of the pages.
\* read_times [ ] is an array that records read times of the pages.

---

To locate the PTE and check the *__access_bit* of each page during the samplings, SysMon needs to lookup virtual address layer by layer (see Fig. 1). In consideration of the fact that all pages targeted by a request are virtually contiguous, most of their PTEs are adjacent. It means that SysMon only needs to obtain the first page's PTE from the page table root; for each of the remaining pages, we can get their PTEs by adding a fixed offset without starting from PGD [12]. Traversing like this can reduce the sampling overhead.

For the running applications, Algorithm_1 shows the pseudo-code for obtaining the page access frequency. In the first loop, SysMon clears all pages' *__access_bit* (Line 2); and then, check the *__access_bit* using function *pte_young()* (Line 6).

**Table 1.** Classification standard for page "heat".

| The number of accesses | Page "Heat" | The number of accesses | Page "Heat" |
|---|---|---|---|
| Larger than 200 | Very High | 64–100 | Low |
| 150–200 | High | 10–64 | Lower |
| 100–150 | Medium | Less than 10 | Very low |

After 200 samplings, SysMon will calculate the total number of accesses of each page, and grade pages according to the page "heat" (i.e., the number of accesses). Classification standard in our experiments is shown in Table 1. It can be adjusted according to the characteristics of workloads. In addition, SysMon can calculate the memory footprint of the running workload.

### 3.3    Module 2: Write/Read Operations Statistics

SysMon dynamically monitors the write/read operations of hot pages during samplings. In the page classification process (see Fig. 3), we give write operations a heavier weight as write operations are more expensive than read operations in memory system (i.e., empirical value is 2 since write operations need to read data, modify and write back to the memory, causing a longer latency than read operations [29]). And this value can be adjusted according to the specific environments and configurations.

Algorithm_1 shows how to calculate the write/read times of each page. SysMon clear the __access_bit and __dirty_bit in the first loop (Line 2); and in the second loop, if *pte_dirty()* returns 1, it means write operation occurs. Otherwise, a read operation is detected (Lines 8–12). Moreover, SysMon can also record that, compared with the last sampling, the number of write pages converting into read pages and the number of read pages converting into write pages. It is meaningful for the data placement that distinguishes the page is a write domain page or a read domain page.

### 3.4    Module 3: Re-use Time Statistics

In order to calculate re-use time of a page, SysMon monitors whether this page is accessed in each sampling, and uses an array to record the interval between the two accesses, this is so-called "re-use time" of that page. Figure 4 denotes the re-use time of the selected page, where *iterations* means the samplings, and *access times* records the picked page's access times. Algorithm_2 describes how to calculate the re-use time of a page. SysMon checks the __access_bit, if the page is accessed, the number of accesses *times* adds 1; if not, the re-use "distance" between last access and next access increases 1 (Lines 6–10).

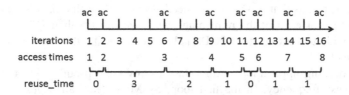

**Fig. 4.** Re-use time of one page.

---

**Algorithm_2:** Calculate Re-Use Time
**Input:** The NO. of page P **Output:** reuse_time [ ]

---

1. **FOR** i **FROM** 0 **TO** ITERATIONS // default 200
2. **DO**
3.   Clear __*access_bit* of page P;
4.   Obtain PTE of page P via P's address;
5.   **IF** pte_present (PTE) **THEN**   // P is in the memory
6.     **IF** pte_yong (PTE) **THEN**   // P has been accessed
7.       times ← times + 1;
8.     **ELSE**   // P has not been accessed
9.       reuse_time [times] ← reuse_time [times] + 1;
10.    **END IF**
11.  **END IF**
12. **END FOR**
13. **RETURN** reuse_time [ ];

---

\* times is used to record the access times of the page P.
\* reuse_time [ ] records the re-use time of page P.

---

**Algorithm_3:** Bank Hotness Statistics
**Output:** bank_hotness [ ]

---

1. #define BANKBITS_1   (0x600)   // 21, 22 bits
2. #define BANKBITS_2   (0xE)   // 13, 14, 15 bits
3. #define PAGE_TO_BANK   ((page_to_pfn (page) & (BANKBITS_1))
                  >> 6 | ((page_to_pfn (page) & (BANKBITS_2)) >> 1
4. **FOR** i **FROM** 0 **TO** ITERATIONS **DO**// default 200
5.   Clear __*access_bit* of all pages;
6.   **FOR** each page P **IN** an application **DO**
7.     Obtain PTE of page P via P's address;
8.     **IF** pte_present (PTE) **THEN**   // P is in the memory
9.       **IF** pte_yong (PTE) **THEN**   // P has been accessed
10.        bank_id ← PAGE_TO_BANK (pte_page (PTE));
11.        bank_hotness [bank_id] ← bank_hotness [bank_id] + 1;
12.      **END IF**
13.    **END IF**
14.   **END FOR**
15. **END FOR**
16. **RETURN** bank_hotness [ ]

---

\* PAGE_TO_BANK is a Macro definition that returns the bank_id
  according to Page Frame Number (PFN).
\* bank_hotness [ ] records the number of hot pages in each bank.

---

The pages to be monitored are chosen randomly before samplings. By doing so, SysMon guarantees that there is less deviation when collecting re-use time information during samplings. Page-level re-use time information is an important factor that reflects the application access behaviors, which represents the temporal locality of the pages. By analyzing the re-use time, we can quantify how quickly the particular pages will be accessed again. Taking re-use time into account can accurately reflect the page access trend and the applications' overall memory access trend during the period of time.

### 3.5    Module 4: Bank Hotness Statistics

The main memory system is composed of several DRAM banks that are shared by multiple running processes. When several requests from different process falling on the same DRAM bank, the access conflict occurs, and these requests have to be handled in a sequential order. This causes row buffer thrashing and a longer access delay, and declines the overall performance of the system. Therefore, it is the foundation of further optimizing memory scheduling algorithms to clearly understand the bank hotness/balance information among several DRAM banks.

As illustrated in Algorithm_3, SysMon calculates the number of hot pages in each bank. *PAGE_TO_BANK* is a macro definition that can extract the bank bits and obtain the bank id (Line 3). Note that Algorithm_3 is implemented with channel interleaving under the configuration of Fig. 2(a). When the entire bandwidth demand is larger than 2 GB/s, channel partition is more effective and can avoid significant performance degradation [15]. In the case above, since there are 64 banks in the memory system (32 banks/per channel), *PAGE_TO_BANK* should simultaneously extract channel bit and bank bits to calculate the bank id.

## 4    Optimization

For the applications that need large memory footprint, to reduce the scanning over-head during samplings, SysMon randomly scans a portion of pages instead of traversing all the Virtual Memory Areas (VMAs). As illustrated in Fig. 5, SysMon scans 5% pages in our experiments. Before sampling, SysMon generates a random number as the sampling's starting point within a VMA by using function *get_random_bytes()*. The sampling interval of pages can be calculated by scanning ratio (i.e., 1/0.05 = 20 in our experiments). The scanning ratio can be adjusted as required.

**Fig. 5.** SysMon samples a portion of pages to analyze the applications' behaviors. Note that the sampling fraction here is only for illustration purpose. In our experiments, we sample 5% of pages during each sampling.

To reduce the error efficiently, SysMon uses different random numbers before each sampling. After 200 samplings, all the pages can be covered. We adopt equal interval sampling (i.e., sample page 0, 20, 40, 60…) instead of completely random design (i.e., generate random numbers constantly as the page number during samplings). It is because if we use the second method, we have to record all the random numbers, so the space overhead will increase linearly as the memory footprint increases; it is contrary to the intention of "randomization to reduce the sampling overhead", and not worth the candle.

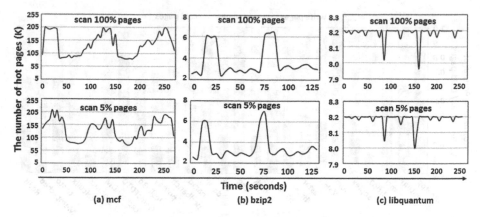

**Fig. 6.** The number of hot pages by using random sampling method.

Our experiments show that sample 5% pages can accurately reflect the applications' memory access trend, the ratio of hot pages, etc. Figure 6 gives several examples of benchmarks. Experiments show that randomization can reduce the scanning overhead by 33.12% at least (tonto), 47.89% at most (Memcached), and 44.42% on average.

## 5 Evaluation

### 5.1 How to Run SysMon

We study SysMon on the configuration of Fig. 2(a). To run SysMon, we firstly need to write a *Makefile* file. Each source file (i.e., *\*.c*) corresponds to a line "obj-m += *\*.o*" in the *Makefile*. After using *make* command to compile the source files, we then use *insmod \*.ko* command to insert the module into the kernel. Finally, use *dmesg* to output the results.

### 5.2 Benchmarks

We evaluate SysMon with diverse workloads, including SPECCPU2006, widely used Memcached with data from Twitter and Redis. SPECCPU2006 benchmark is an industry-standardized, CPU-intensive benchmark suite. The widely used Memcached is a distributed memory object caching system. It is an in-memory key-value store for small chunks of arbitrary data from results of database calls, API calls, or page rendering. Redis is a popular NoSQL database and is single-threaded. Redis has no file I/O after loading the dataset into memory.

### 5.3 Experimental Results

**Memory Footprint and Write/Read Operations.** Figure 7 shows the benchmarks' average normalized portion of different types of pages (i.e., write page, read page and

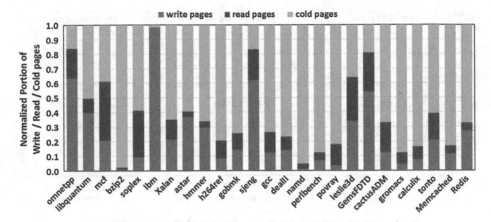

**Fig. 7.** Normalized portion of the three types of pages of different benchmarks.

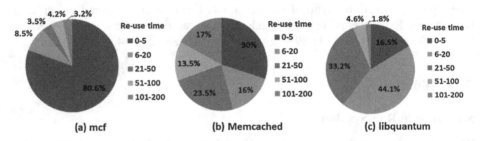

**Fig. 8.** Normalized portion of different re-use time sections.

cold page). It can be seen from Fig. 7 that more than 80% pages of omnetpp, sjeng, lbm and GemsFDTD are hot pages; more than 90% pages of lbm are write pages. For bzip2 and namd, less than 10% pages are hot pages. As for Memcached and Redis, though their memory footprints are large, the portion of hot pages/active pages is not that large.

**Re-use Time.** We tested all the benchmarks and observed that there are two categories can be classified by the re-use time characteristics. One is that most re-use times are relatively small; the other is the re-use times are evenly distributed in different sections.

Figure 8 represents the portion of different re-use time sections. Figure 8(a) shows that for mcf, 80.6% re-use time (i.e., re-use distance) is less than 5, and only 7.4% re-use time is larger than 50 within 200 samplings; it means that the memory access for mcf is very intensive. Libquantum (Fig. 8(c)) is similar to mcf, most re-use times are between 0 and 20, only 6.4% re-use time is larger than 50. As for Memcached (Fig. 8 (b)), the re-use time distribution is more balanced, which indicated that memory access is not that intensive compared with mcf and libquantum.

**Bank Hotness.** Figure 9 illustrates the normalized hot page number (i.e., bank hotness) within each DRAM bank. By exploring the bank hotness of all benchmarks, we found that the hot page distribution is not balanced in many cases. Taking Memcached

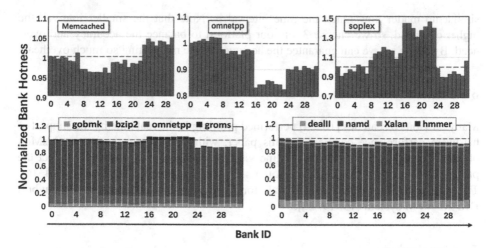

**Fig. 9.** Normalized bank hotness of single benchmark and multi-benchmarks.

as an example, the hottest bank (bank 31) has 531 more hot pages than the coldest bank (bank 15). Besides, we randomly choose two workloads and test their bank hotness. To eliminate the bank unbalance, Liu et al. [17] proposes a page-coloring based bank-level partition mechanism, which allocates specific DRAM banks to specific threads.

## 5.4  Sampling Interval

In our experiments, the sampling interval between two sampling periods is set to 3 s. In terms of the time interval, we are challenged by a question: how much the interval should we use to obtain the applications' memory access information with low overhead and good accuracy? To study the relation between sampling accuracy and sampling interval, we test the hot page numbers of all benchmarks by using different intervals (i.e., 1 s, 3 s, 5 s, and 7 s). Due to the space limitation, we show two benchmarks in Fig. 10. It can be seen that the variation trends of hot page numbers are

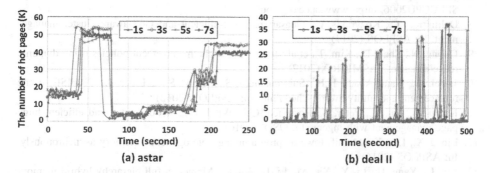

**Fig. 10.** The number of hot pages under the configuration of different sampling intervals.

similar no matter how much the time interval is. Note that the smaller interval, the higher overhead, so we choose 3 s in our platform to balance the accuracy and overhead. By doing so, we can guarantee the accuracy while not costing so much overhead.

## 6  Related Work

Many previous researches [10, 24] performed profiling in the real time by the support of hardware performance counters. In this paper, without hardware supports, SysMon obtains memory access behaviors online via OS approach, and is able to collect the page-level re-use time, bank balance/hotness, and the write/read characteristics [14, 16]. The captured information is critical for the memory management on hybrid DRAM-NVM system [13, 19, 22].

## 7  Conclusion

This paper re-designs SysMon as a Linux kernel module to meet the challenges on monitoring large memory footprint applications. To balance the sampling overhead and accuracy, we adopt a random sampling method and explore the appropriate sampling interval. Experiments show that 44.42% sampling overhead on average can be reduced by using random sampling method. We capture a large number of benchmarks' memory behaviors including page access frequency, write/read and hot/cold features, re-use time and bank balance/hotness by using SysMon.

## References

1. Memcached. http://memcached.org
2. Oprofile. http://oprofile.sourceforge.net/news/
3. PAPI. http://icl.utk.edu/papi/
4. Perfmon2. http://perfmon2.sourceforge.net/
5. Pin. https://software.intel.com/en-us/articles/pin-a-dynamic-binary-instrumentation-tool
6. Redis. http://redis.io/
7. SPECCPU2006. http://www.spec.org/cpu2006
8. Delimitrou, C., Kozyrakis, C.: Quasar: resource-efficient and QoS-aware cluster management. In: ASPLOS (2014)
9. Duong, N., Zhao, D., Kim, T., et al.: Improving cache management policies using dynamic reuse distances. In: MICRO (2012)
10. Jaleel, A., Najaf-Abadi, H.H., Subramaniam, S., Steely, S.C., Emer, J.: CRUISE: cache replacement and utility-aware scheduling. In: ASPLOS (2012)
11. Kwon, Y., Yu, H., Peter, S., Rossbach, C.J., Witchel, E.: Coordinated and efficient huge page management with ingens. In: OSDI (2016)
12. Lin, F.X., Liu, X.: Memif: towards programming heterogeneous memory asynchronously. In: ASPLOS (2016)
13. Liu, L., Yang, H., Li, Y., Xie, M., Li, L. Wu, C.: Memos: a full hierarchy hybrid memory management framework. In: ICCD (2016)

14. Liu, L., Li, Y., Ding, C., Yang, H., Wu, C.: Rethinking memory management in modern operating system: horizontal, vertical or random? TC **65**, 1926–1935 (2016)
15. Liu, L., Cui, Z., Li, Y., et al.: BPM/BPM+: software-based dynamic memory partitioning mechanisms for mitigating DRAM bank-/channel-level interferences in multicore systems. ACM Trans. Archit. Code Optim. (TACO) **11**(1), 5 (2014)
16. Liu, L., Li, Y., Cui, Z., Wu, C., et al.: Going vertical in memory management: handling multiplicity by multi-policy. In: ISCA (2014)
17. Liu, L., Cui, Z., Xing, M., Wu, C., et al.: A software memory partition approach for eliminating bank-level interference in multicore systems. In: PACT (2012)
18. Lee, S., Bahn, H., Noh, S.H.: CLOCK-DWF: a write-history-aware page replacement algorithm for hybrid PCM and DRAM memory architectures. TC **63**, 2187–2200 (2014)
19. Liu, L., Xie, M., Yang, H.: Memos: revisiting hybrid memory management in modern operating system. arXiv:1703.07725 (2017)
20. Lv, F., Liu, L., et al.: WiseThrottling: a new asynchronous task scheduler for mitigating I/O bottleneck in large-scale datacenter servers. J. Supercomput. **71**, 3054–3093 (2015)
21. Lv, F., Cui, H., Wang, L., Liu, L., et al.: Dynamic I/O-aware scheduling for batch-mode applications on chip multiprocessor systems of cluster platforms. JCST **29**, 21–37 (2014)
22. Liu, L.: Tackling diversity and heterogeneity by vertical memory management. arXiv:1704.01198 (2017)
23. Liang, Y., Li, X.: Efficient kernel management on GPUs. ACM Trans. Embed. Comput. Syst. (TECS) **16**(4), 115 (2017)
24. Mai, H.T., Park, K.H., Lee, H.S., Kim, C.S., Lee, M., Hur, S.J.: Dynamic data migration in hybrid main memories for in-memory big data storage. ETRI J. **36**, 988–998 (2014)
25. Mutlu, O.: Main memory scaling: challenges and solution directions. In: Topaloglu, R. (ed.) More than Moore Technologies for Next Generation Computer Design, pp. 127–153. Springer, New York (2015). doi:10.1007/978-1-4939-2163-8_6
26. Rixner, S., Dally, W.J., Kapasi, U.J., et al.: Memory access scheduling. ACM SIGARCH Comput. Archit. News **28**(2), 128–138 (2000). ACM
27. Sun, G., Zhang, C., Li, P., et al.: Statistical cache bypassing for non-volatile memory. IEEE Trans. Comput. **65**(11), 3427–3440 (2016)
28. Mi, W., Feng, X., Xue, J., Jia, Y.: Software-hardware cooperative DRAM bank partitioning for chip multiprocessors. In: Ding, C., Shao, Z., Zheng, R. (eds.) NPC 2010. LNCS, vol. 6289, pp. 329–343. Springer, Heidelberg (2010). doi:10.1007/978-3-642-15672-4_28
29. Kim, Y., Seshadri, V., Lee, D., Liu, J., Mutlu, O.: A case for exploiting subarray-level parallelism (SALP) in DRAM. ACM SIGARCH Comput. Archit. News **40**(3), 368–379 (2012)

# Self-adaptive Failure Detector for Peer-to-Peer Distributed System Considering the Link Faults

Yanzhang He, Xiaohong Jiang$^{(\boxtimes)}$, Changbo Dai, and Zikun Fan

College of Computer Science, Zhejiang University, Hangzhou 310027, China
{heyanzhang, jiangxh, daichangbo, fanzikun}@zju.edu.cn

**Abstract.** Nowadays, the distributed computing is prevailing in artificial intelligence applications due to the limited computation capacity of single computing node. Generally, distributed computing system contains large scale of computing node, and therefore system breakdown is regarded as usual matter. To enhance the system availability and performance, failure detection dominates important status to recover the system. The traditional failure detector simply equates the link fault with the node fault problem, which greatly affects the resource utilization, fault locating and fast repair. We present a self-adaptive Link-based Failure Detection Agreement DLFDA with an improved node fault detection algorithm, which can accurately distinguish the node fault and link fault. DLFDA can dynamically adjust the detection structure to increase the coverage of the link fault detection, while using *Gossip* protocol to distribute fault diagnosis results to other system members, which extensively reduces the damage of the system performance. Finally, the experimental results show that our method can meet the requirements of theoretical design.

**Keywords:** Distributed system · Failure detector · Self-adaptive · Link fault · Node fault

## 1 Introduction

With the development of distributed technology, the distributed system is prevailing in multiple cloud computing and artificial intelligence applications, such as HPACS [1], Hadoop virtual cluster [2], AlphaGo, medical intelligent diagnosis and smart cars, which can provide high performance and availability service compared with traditional single node computing. However, with the increasing of the system scale, which always contains thousands of computing nodes, the system breakdown is regarded as usual matter. For instance, On April 21, 2011, EC2 suffered a customer-impacting service disruption in the US East Region, which leads to about 75 websites be not accessible [3]. Also, Microsoft Outlook.com experienced large-scale downtime in 2013, and even cause some users can not use the service within three days, seriously affecting the service quality and user experience [4].

To improve the performance and availability in the distributed system, timely and effective system failure detection is critical, and we must deal with two fundamental challenges: fault tolerance and asynchronism [5]. Fault tolerance is an important goal of distributed system design, which is an important means to improve the system's

© Springer International Publishing AG 2017
Y. Dou et al. (Eds.): APPT 2017, LNCS 10561, pp. 64–75, 2017.
DOI: 10.1007/978-3-319-67952-5_6

autonomous operation and fault immunity [6]. It can guarantee the correct operation in the case of partial failure of the system, and will not greatly influence the overall system performance. Fault detection, as one of the basic components of system availability, provides the basis for triggering failure recovery mechanism [7], and is a prerequisite for fault tolerance. However, the asynchronism of the distributed system can not warrant the accuracy of fault detection. In asynchronous systems, the processing speed of the *Process* and the delay of the message transmission between different processes are not bounded. The system can't differentiate the reasons when it fails to receive the heartbeat message, such as the network transmission delay, slow processing speed of the *Process*, or process failure.

At present, most failure detection agreements simply regard the link fault as the node fault, that is, whatever it is the node fault or link fault, it is determined that the node connected to the link is faulty, which will result in low resource utilization of the system. While some other failure detection methods prevent the waste of resources by tolerating link faults, but this tolerance can lead to serious errors in the entire distributed system. The contributions of this paper can be summarized as follows:

- First, we propose a self-adaptive Link-based Failure Detection Agreement DLFDA with an improved node fault detection algorithm, which can not only detect the node fault, but also distinguish the link fault in the system. DLFDA judges the fault type through the analysis of multiple detectors located in different nodes of the distributed system;
- Second, DLFDA can dynamically adjust the detection structure to increase the coverage of the link fault detection, and using *Gossip* protocol to distribute fault diagnosis results, which reduces the decrease of the system performance;
- At last, we implement the DLFDA and conduct a lot of experiments. The experimental results show that our method can meet the requirements of theoretical design.

The rest of this paper is structured as follows. In Sect. 2, we give the introduction of related works. In Sect. 3, we first present topological structure of DLFDA, then we explain the execution steps of DLFDA, including improved node fault detector, judgment of fault type, diagnosis result distribution and system detection structure adjustment. The Sect. 4 shows the experiment and result analysis. In the last section, we conclude our work.

## 2 Related Work

Failure detection technology has been accompanied by the development of distributed systems, and it is one of the most important components to build a reliable distributed system. Since the failure detection technology was proposed, many researchers have been paying close attention to it, and a variety of failure detector were proposed to meet the different needs. Such as the Byzantine Generals problem [8] proposed by Leslie Lamport, who is a Turing Award winner and expert in the distributed technology field. Failure detection is one of the most important means to ensure fault tolerance of distributed systems, and it is first defined by Chandra and Toueg [9]. In addition, two important attributes are defined in the paper to measure the detection capability of the fault detector. "Completeness" is used to measure the ability to eventually detect each fault in the system, and the "Accuracy" is used to measure the ability to correctly detect the fault process.

Heartbeat protocol and ping protocol always used in the failure detector. The heartbeat protocol is generally used to negotiate and monitor the availability of a resource, which includes pull-mode and push-mode message communication. The heartbeat protocol can detect the status of Process granularity, while the ping protocol can only detect the status of computing node granularity. The $\varphi$-FD is the earliest well-known heartbeat based failure detector proposed by Hayashibara et al. [10, 11], which includes fault monitoring and interpretation, and provides a cumulative value based on heartbeat interval variation. The $\varphi$-FD uses push-mode heartbeat detection technology to maintains a sliding window of size $n$ to store the heartbeat messages in the detection process, and has an effective design with the simple calculation of the output value $\varphi$. The premise of the $\varphi$-FD is to assume that the heartbeat arrival interval is a normal distribution. When the interval between two heartbeats increases or decreases, the value of $\varphi$ increases or decreases at the same time, which indicates that the possibility of system failure raises or declines. At present, many distributed systems failure detector are based on $\varphi$-FD, such as open source Apache distributed NoSQL database Cassandra [12], and distributed application framework Akka. Cassandra system used the exponential distribution to replace the normal distribution in the detector, simplifying the calculation of $\varphi$ value. Bjm-FD [9] improves the $\varphi$-FD, and uses the cumulative distribution of the heartbeat messages in the sliding window to further simplify the calculation of $\varphi$ value, and to make the failure detector be more accurate in the network environment with heavy packet loss. The failure detectors mentioned above have simple and flexible structure. However, they can't differentiate the link fault and node fault, and the link fault is simply regarded as the node fault, which can't satisfy the "Accuracy".

The SWIM protocol [13] is an extensible, weakly consistent protocol, which is suitable for decentralized distributed system such as P2P architecture. The protocol tolerates the link fault in the system through the "re-detection" mechanism. When one node member can't ping another node member, it sets it as a suspected computing node. Then it randomly chooses some other node members to re-detect the suspected node, if it doesn't receive *ack* message from other computing node members after a period time, it can judge the suspected node as faulty node. Horita et al. [14] improved the "re-detection" mechanism by using the static configuration to choose the other node members, and it can reduce the time complexity. However, the SWIM and the improved protocols uses ping instead of heartbeat, so it can not refine the detection granularity of to the process, instead of computing node. They also ignore the link fault, which can't satisfy the "Completeness", and will result in system error and low system performance. We aim to propose a self-adaptive link-based failure detection agreement to meet the not only the "Accuracy", but also the "Completeness".

## 3  Description of DLFDA

We can describe the distributed system as a grape $G$ with $n$ nodes and $l$ edges $G = (V, E)$. $V$ is the set of nodes, and can be regarded as Processes running in different nodes $\{P_1, P_2, P_3, \ldots, P_n\}$. $E$ is the set of edges, and $E = \{p, q | \forall p, q \in V, p \neq q\}$, which means all Processes are interconnected over the network link. Each Process maintains a system member list $list_1$ and a link list $list_2$, and sorts the system member list and link list by the value of $hash(P_i)$. The hash code is calculated by the unique ID of $P_i$, and to ensure that the hash code of different Processes will not repeat. To simplify the description, we can presume the ID numbers are continuous positive integers, and the Fig. 1 shows an example. When the Process receives the failure Gossip message from other Processes, it will update the system member list and link list. The execution steps of DLFDA includes 4 modules: improved node fault detector, fault type judgment, diagnosis result distribution and system detection structure adjustment.

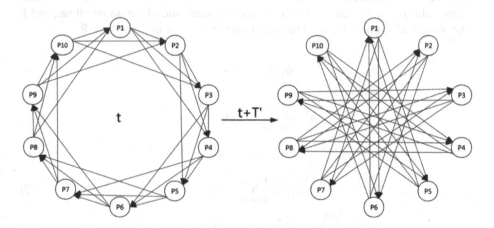

**Fig. 1.** Detection topology in DLFDA method

### 3.1  Improved Node Fault Detector

In order to void serious detection load to the system performance by failure detection, we need to reduce the quantity of heartbeat messages at the same time. In DLFDA, we don't use all-to-all way to detect, and use the detection topology shown in Fig. 1 to reduce the amount of detection heartbeat messages. At the time $t$, the process $P_i$ detects the following $1 \sim k$ processes, and changes to detect $k+1 \sim 2k$ processes after the interval $T'$. Theoretically, it needs to take $(n * T')/2k$ to detect all the links in the system, which the link quantity is $n * (n - 1)/2$. DLFDA uses improved node fault detector DA-FD to calculate the $\varphi$ value between Processes. DA-FD maintains a $n$ size practical historical heartbeat interval sequence and a $n$ size estimated historical heartbeat interval sequence to calculate the exponential moving average value. The calculation of $\varphi$ is showed as formula 1. $t_{now}$ is the current time, and $T_{last}$ is the time of last heartbeat.

$$\varphi(t_{now}) = e^{\frac{t_{now} - T_{last}}{EIA_{\ell+1} + \alpha_{\ell+1}}} - 1 \tag{1}$$

$EIA_{\ell+1}$ is the estimation interval value of the next heartbeat and the $\alpha_{\ell+1}$ is the average error value of the former $n$ times of estimation. $EIA_{\ell+1}$ and $\alpha_{\ell+1}$ can be calculated by formula 2 and 3.

$$EIA_{\ell+1} = \frac{\sum_{i=0}^{n-1} (1-\beta)^i \psi(v_{n-i}) IA_{n-i}}{\sum_{i=0}^{n-1} (1-\beta)^i \psi(v_{n-i})} \tag{2}$$

$$\alpha_{\ell+1} = \frac{1}{n} \sum_{i=0}^{n-1} (IA_i - EIA_i) \tag{3}$$

where $IA_i$ is the practical interval value of the $i$ th heartbeat, $EIA_i$ is the estimated interval value of the $i$th heartbeat, $\psi(v_i)$ is the variance ratio of the $i$th heartbeat, and $\beta$ is the weight adjustment factor. The calculation is showed in formula 4–8.

$$\psi(v_i) = \frac{\delta^2}{\delta^2 + v_i^2} \tag{4}$$

$$\delta^2 = \frac{1}{n} \sum_{i=1}^{n} (IA_i - \mu)^2 \tag{5}$$

$$v_i = IA_i - \mu \tag{6}$$

$$\mu = \frac{1}{n} \sum_{i=1}^{n} IA_i \tag{7}$$

$$\beta = \frac{2}{N+1}, N \leq \frac{n}{3.45} - 1 \tag{8}$$

We can see that DA-FD does not need to assume that the heartbeat arrival intervals obey the normal distribution, and does not need to calculate the cumulative probability of the distribution. When the $\varphi$ value exceeds the value of threshold, then it judge the $P_j$ as suspected Process and invokes the fault type judgment module in the Sect. 3.2.

When $P_i$ receives the heartbeat message before the $\varphi$ value increases to the threshold, then it can judge the $P_j$ as normal Process. Table 1 shows the pseudo-code of the improved node fault detection algorithm.

**Table 1.** Pseudo-code of DA-FD

---

1. At time $\eta, 2\eta, 3\eta, ...,$ process $P_i$ send heartbeat request to process $P_j$, and the heartbeat response messages are $m_1, m_2, m_3,....$
2. Initialization:
3. $\quad n, threshold$ = init value; // set the size of moving sliding window and the threshold value.
4. $\quad queue_1 = empty(n);$
5. $\quad queue_2 = empty(n);$// create two queues to store the practical and estimated interval value of heartbeats.
6. while($t_{now}$)
7. $\quad EIA_{\ell+1} = \frac{\sum_{i=0}^{n-1}(1-\beta)^i\psi(v_{n-i})IA_{n-i}}{\sum_{i=0}^{n-1}(1-\beta)^i\psi(v_{n-i})}$ ;// calculate the estimated interval value of next heartbeat.
8. $\quad \alpha_{\ell+1} = \frac{1}{n}\sum_{i=0}^{n-1}(IA_i - EIA_i)$ ;
9. $\quad \varphi(t_{now}) = e^{\frac{t_{now}-T_{last}}{EIA_{\ell+1}+\alpha_{\ell+1}}} - 1$ ; // calculate the $\varphi$ value of next heartbeat.
10. $\quad$ if $\varphi(t_{now}) \geq theshold$ then
11. $\quad\quad$ suspect( $P_j$ );
12. $\quad$ if receive $m_k$ at $t_{now}$ then
13. $\quad\quad T_{last} = t_{now};$
14. $\quad\quad queue1.add(t - T_{last});$
15. $\quad\quad queue2.add(EIA_{\ell+1});$ // update the queues.

---

## 3.2　Fault Type Judgment

The Fig. 2 shows the link fault detection steps in the DLFDA method. The Process $P_i$ sends a heartbeat detection message to the process $P_j$. If there is no heartbeat response received within a certain period of time, the $\varphi$ value calculated by Sect. 3.1 exceeds the threshold value. In this case, we can't judge $P_j$ as node fault or link fault. It spreads the message of "suspect($P_j$)" state to other $k-1$ detectors. After the Processes $\{P_{S1}, P_{S2}, ..., P_{si}, P_{s(k-1)}\}$ receive the message, they will respond to $P_i$ according to their own detection results. If the result is normal, then $P_i$ can judge the failure as link fault: Failure$(P_i, P_j)$, and updates the link list. If the result is abnormal, then $P_i$ can judge the failure as node fault: Failure$(P_j)$, and invokes the detection result distribution module in the Sect. 3.3. Table 2 show the pseudo-code of fault type judgment.

## 3.3　Diagnosis Result Distribution

The $P_i$ updates the $list_1$ or $list_2$, and distribute the failure$(P_j)$ or failure$(P_i, P_j)$ message to other Processes by Gossip protocol. Gossip distribution protocol is different from the all-to-all distribution mode, the principle is similar to rumors spread, which can reduce the quantity of message transmission and reduce the influence of distributed system performance. Every gossip message has a version number, the other member compares

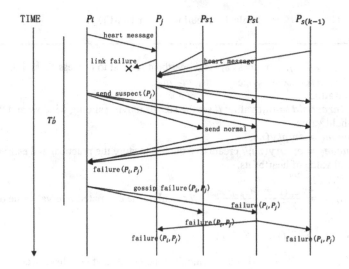

**Fig. 2.** Steps of fault type judgment

**Table 2.** Pseudo-code of fault type judge

| | |
|---|---|
| 1. | if $P_i$ suspect $P_j$ then |
| 2. | $S =$ search (other detector members of $P_j$); //search the Processes of $\{P_{S_1}, P_{S_2}, ..., P_{S_{k-1}}\}$ |
| 3. | send suspect($P_j$) to $S$; |
| 4. | if receive suspect($P_j$) from $P_i$; |
| 5. | if state$(P_j)$ == failure then |
| 6. | nothing; |
| 7. | else |
| 8. | send normal to $P_i$; |
| 9. | if $t > T_b'$ && doesn't receive any response from $S$ then |
| 10. | failure($P_j$); |
| 11. | update($list_1$); |
| 12. | gossip failure($P_j$) ; // distribute failure message to the system members by Gossip protocol. |
| 13. | else if receive normal from $S$ then |
| 14. | failure($P_i, P_j$) ; |
| 15. | update($list_2$); |
| 16. | gossip failure($P_i, P_j$) ; |

it with the local list status when receives the message and merges the latest message. Although the failure message consistency among different Processes can not be guaranteed, all the members can eventually know which node or link is failure. Each member who receive the message update the status of the $list_1$ or $list_2$, and will randomly choose $k$ members who didn't receive the message to send. The steps of diagnosis result distribution can be described as Table 3.

**Table 3.** Diagnosis result distribution by Gossip protocol

| |
|---|
| 1.   receive failure($P_i$) as a gossip $msg$ from other; |
| 2.   $msg$ = update local $list_1$ with failure($P_i$) ; |
| 3.   receive failure($P_i, P_j$) as a gossip $msg$ from other; |
| 4.   $msg$ = update local $list_2$ with failure($P_i, P_j$) ; |
| 5.   $S$ = randomly select several Processes from $list_1$; |
| 6.   Gossip msg to $S$; |

### 3.4 System Detection Structure Adjustment

As shown in Fig. 1, the process $P_i$ detects the following $1 \sim k$ processes at the time $t$, and changes to detect $k+1 \sim 2k$ processes after the interval $T'$. The purpose of structure adjustment is to ensure that all the fault links can be found in a certain period. In the peer-to-peer distributed system, one system member (leader) is required to initiate a detection structure adjustment request in every detection period. For example, the first member of the ordered member list is selected as the initiator. After completing the present fault detection period, the leader notifies the other members in the distributed system to rotate the detection object. After all the members receive the request, they begin to adjust the structure. When the leader is downtime, they will vote the next member of the ordered member list as the leader. The steps of detection structure adjustment can be described as Table 4.

**Table 4.** Steps of detection structure adjustment

| |
|---|
| 1.   if $t - lastT = T'$ then |
| 2.   if $P$ is first process then |
| 3.         send change to other; |
| 4.   else |
| 5.         receive change; |
| 6.         change detection structure; |

## 4   Experimental Results and Analysis

In this section, we first validate the DA-FD algorithm used in DLFDA. In order to compare the failure detection performance, we implement the $\varphi$-FD algorithm and the Bjm-FD algorithm respectively, which are commonly used classical failure detectors mentioned in the related works. Then we implement the DLFDA protocol to verify the detection results of node fault and link fault. Finally, we analyze the advantages of DLFDA protocol.

### 4.1    Result Analysis of DA-FD Algorithm

The Fig. 3 shows the failure detection mistake rate in different threshold value. We set the heartbeat request interval as 100 ms, and compare the result in three different sliding window sizes, $n = 50, n = 200$ and $n = 500$. We can see that the detection mistake rate decreases when the threshold increases, and the rate can be close to 0 when the threshold is infinite. In addition, when the window size is $n = 200$, the mistake rate is significantly lower than $n = 50$, but it is close to the result of $n = 500$. So the sliding window size can increase the accuracy of detection, but when the size increases to a certain extent, the improvement of accuracy rate is not obvious.

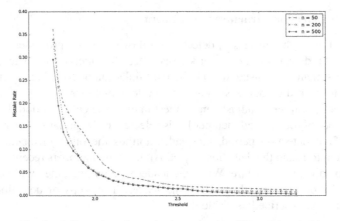

**Fig. 3.** Failure detection mistake rate with different threshold

In order to compare the three algorithms, we use the accuracy rate with the same detection time as the unified evaluation indicator. The detection time is calculated the same as $\varphi$-FD algorithm. We set the heartbeat request interval as 100 ms, and the rate of message loss rate as 0. As shown in Fig. 4, we can see that the mistake rate of all

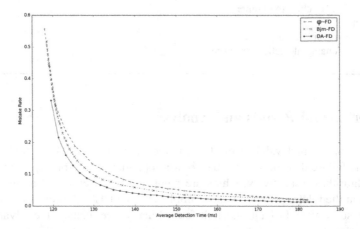

**Fig. 4.** Result comparison of three failure detector algorithms

algorithms gradually reduce with the detection time increases. In addition, when the average detection time is the same, DA-FD algorithm has the lowest mistake rate, better than $\varphi$-FD and Bjm-FD.

Finally, to verify the performance of DA-FD in high message loss rate network environment. We set the heartbeat request interval as 100 ms, and the rate of message loss rate as 1%. As shown in Fig. 5, it can be found that the performance decrease of $\varphi$-FD is higher than the DA-FD and Bjm-FD, which means the $\varphi$-FD is not suitable in the network environment with high message loss. In addition, the accuracy of the DA-FD algorithm is still higher than that of the Bjm-FD algorithm.

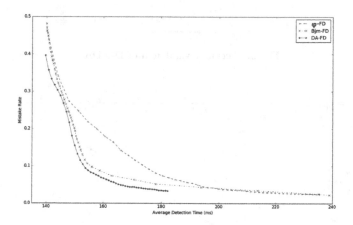

**Fig. 5.** Result comparison with message loss

## 4.2   Validation of DLFDA

First, we need to verify the efficiency of DLFDA for link fault detection. In the experiment, we set the heartbeat request interval as 100 ms, and the threshold of DA-FD algorithm is 3. We use the *iptables* command in the Linux operating system to simulate the link fault. As shown in Fig. 6, when the number of detection nodes is $k = 1$, the link fault rate is 100%, which means the link fault is equivalent to node fault. When $k > 1$, the detection mistake rate is gradually reduced by the detection time. In addition, when the $k$ increases, the detection mistake rate is relatively reduced, this is because more detection nodes can be more timely detect the node fault and link fault.

Finally, we analyze the impact of DLFDA protocol on system performance, which means the analysis of the detection message load in unit time. As shown in Fig. 7, the detection message load is related to the value of $k$. Unlike the all-to-all mode failure detection, the detection message load is $O(n)$, rather than $O(n^2)$.

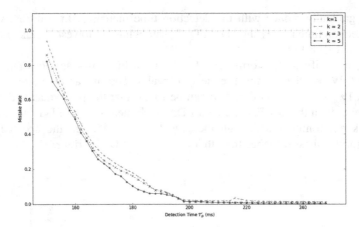

**Fig. 6.** Accuracy validation of DLFDA

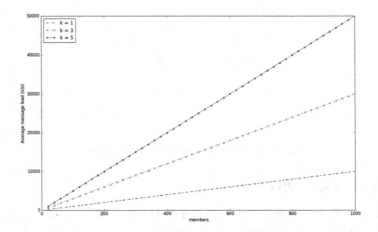

**Fig. 7.** Detection load of DLFDA

## 5 Conclusions

To solve the weaknesses of $\varphi$-FD and Bjm-FD, we propose a more flexible DA-FD algorithm with higher efficiency. The DA-FD algorithm doesn't need the hypothesis of normal distribution, which is more efficient and less affected by the sliding window size. The experiments show that DA-FD has better performance than $\varphi$-FD and Bjm-FD in all network situations.

To differentiate the link fault and node fault, we propose a self-adaptive Link-based Failure Detection Agreement DLFDA. DLFDA can not only detect the node fault, but also distinguish the link fault in the system. DLFDA judges the fault type through the analysis of multiple detectors located in different nodes of the distributed system. DLFDA can dynamically adjust the detection structure to increase the coverage of the link fault detection, and using *Gossip* protocol to distribute fault diagnosis results, which reduces the influence of the system performance. The experimental results show that our method can meet the requirements of theoretical design.

**Acknowledgments.** This work is supported by National High Technology Research 863 Major Program of China (No. 2011AA01A207).

# References

1. He, Y., Jiang, X., Ye, K., Ma, R., Li, X.: HPACS: a high privacy and availability cloud storage platform with matrix encryption. In: Wu, C., Cohen, A. (eds.) APPT 2013. LNCS, vol. 8299, pp. 132–145. Springer, Heidelberg (2013). doi:10.1007/978-3-642-45293-2_10
2. He, Y., Jiang, X., Wu, Z., et al.: Scalability analysis and improvement of hadoop virtual cluster with cost consideration. In: IEEE 7th International Conference on Cloud Computing (CLOUD), pp. 594–601. IEEE Press, New York (2014)
3. Summary of the Amazon EC2 and Amazon RDS Service Disruption in the US East Region. https://aws.amazon.com/cn/message/65648/
4. Microsoft apologizes for Outlook, ActiveSync downtime, says error overloaded servers. http://www.theverge.com/2013/8/17/4631622
5. Guerraoui, R., Hurfinn, M., Mostefaoui, A., Oliveira, R., Raynal, M., Schiper, A.: Consensus in asynchronous distributed systems: a concise guided tour. In: Krakowiak, S., Shrivastava, S. (eds.) Advances in Distributed Systems. LNCS, vol. 1752, pp. 33–47. Springer, Heidelberg (2000). doi:10.1007/3-540-46475-1_2
6. Sar, A., Akkaya, M.: Fault tolerance mechanisms in distributed systems. Int. J. Commun. Netw. Syst. Sci. **8**, 471–482 (2015)
7. Pasin, M., Fontaine, S., Bouchenak, S.: Failure detection in large scale systems: a survey. In: Proceedings of IEEE Network Operations and Management Symposium Workshops, pp. 7–11. IEEE Press, New York (2008)
8. Lamport, L., Shostak, R., Pease, M.: The Byzantine generals problem. ACM Trans. Program. Lang. Syst. (TOPLAS) **4**(3), 382–401 (1982)
9. Satzger, B., Pietzowski, A., Trumler, W., et al.: A new adaptive accrual failure detector for dependable distributed systems. In: Proceedings of the 2007 ACM symposium on Applied computing, pp. 551–555. ACM Press, New York (2007)
10. Hayashibara, N., Defago, X., Yared, R., et al.: The φ accrual failure detector. In: Proceedings of the 23rd IEEE International Symposium on Reliable Distributed Systems, pp. 66–78. IEEE Press, New York (2004)
11. Hayashibara, N., Défago, X., Katayama, T.: Two-ways adaptive failure detection with the φ-failure detector. In: Workshop on Adaptive Distributed Systems (WADiS 2003), pp. 22–27. (2003)
12. Apache Cassandra: Apache Cassandra. http://planetcassandra.org/what-is-apache-cassandra
13. Das, A., Gupta, I., Motivala, A.: Swim: Scalable weakly-consistent infection-style process group membership protocol. In: Proceedings of the International Conference on Dependable Systems and Networks (DSN 2002), pp. 303–312. IEEE Press, New York (2002)
14. Horita, Y., Taura, K., Chikayama, T.: A scalable and efficient self-organizing failure detector for grid applications. In: Proceedings of the 6th IEEE/ACM International Workshop on Grid Computing, pp. 202–210. IEEE Computer Society, New York (2005)

# A Survey About Quantitative Measurement of Performance Variability in High Performance Computers

Linping Wu[(⊠)], Xiaowen Xu, Yong Wei, and Xu Liu

High Performance Computing Center,
Institute of Applied Physics and Computational Mathematics,
Beijing 100094, China
wlp@iapcm.ac.cn

**Abstract.** Due to less healthy, contention for shared resources, operating system interference and other factors in high performance computers, there are performance variability phenomena during various components runtime. With the scale of systems and numerical simulation program parallelism increases, the impact of performance variability will be magnified. This will introduce performance variability and degradations, affect applications scalability and overall system throughput. In this context, the performance variability becomes important question for both HPC systems and numerical simulation applications. The future research about this question will be helpful for the system and application design towards future exascale computing. In terms of this issue, this paper gives a literature review about quantitative measurement of performance variability in HPC systems. We summarize the quantitative measurement method of performance variability for three different components, including computation, memory and communication, respectively. Finally, we analyze the gap between researches and challenging demands, potential research issues and future work are also introduced.

**Keywords:** High performance computer · Performance variability · System noise · Bulk synchronous parallel · Collective communication

## 1 Introduction

### 1.1 Performance Variability in HPC Workloads

As HPC systems scale and numerical simulation applications parallelism increased, the performance variability of HPC workloads is common in large-scale parallel computers. For examples, (1) using the same binary code and input files, the performance variability of applications is significantly great while running on different computing nodes group, (2) using the same binary code, input files and nodes, the performance

---

This research is supported by the National Key R&D Plan of China (No. 2016YFBO201403), National Natural Science Foundation of China (61672003).

Y. Dou et al. (Eds.): APPT 2017, LNCS 10561, pp. 76–86, 2017.
DOI: 10.1007/978-3-319-67952-5_7

changes from run to run. The application run-time variability is more and more popular while the parallelism increased. From the system user's perspective, the binary code and input files are unchanged, so the HPC program and input parameter are certain; furthermore, from the numerical simulation software developer's view, the system model of high performance computer is also certain. The program, input parameter and system model are all certain, Why the performance variability exists?

## 1.2 Rout Cause of Performance Variability

With the development of computer architecture and interconnect technology, the peak performance of HPC systems is significantly increased in the past decade. From the TOP500 ranking lists [1], the peak performance of top 1 system increases one order of magnitude every three years. But besides the processor clock speed, the peak performance improvement of HPC systems mainly benefit from the large number of cores because of the Multi- and many core chips. For example, in the latest TOP500 ranking lists (issued on Jun. 2015), the number of cores in every top ten systems are more than 100,000. With now developing trend, future exascale computing platforms consist of $10^8$–$10^9$ cores [2]. The following presents several key characteristics of these systems:

(1) The challenge of scalability toward massive parallelism. The data communication between tasks of parallel application is necessary. The performance variability of any component will cause degraded performance of one task, and other tasks will wait for messages from it. The communication overhead from such wait time will be higher for $10^5$ and future $10^8$ parallelism of the applications.

(2) The contention for shared resources is common. With the node counts and core counts in one node increase, HPC systems might be shared by different applications contending for shared resources (such as CPU cores, processor caches, memory bandwidth, and network bandwidth), and within the same application different requests might contend for resources. The contention for shared resources inevitably results in the performance variability of HPC Workloads.

(3) The network topology can impact application performance in large supercomputers. With the scale of communication network increases, the network topology and the network routing play a very important role and make a precise prediction or modeling of the perturbation hard. In this context, the performance of different tasks in same applications will be variable, and the performance of same applications running on different nodes will be variable from run to run.

(4) There exist the effects of operating system interference on extreme-scale parallel machines. The performance of parallel applications running on large HPC systems is known to degrade due to the interference of kernel and daemon activities on individual nodes, often referred to as operating system noise. Due to the random noise, the performance variability exists during the running time of different tasks in unique application.

(5) Performance degradation is unavoidable as long as a sub-health component is used. In addition to the Fail-Stop [3] faults, some silent errors lead to performance degradation due to the "sub-healthy" state. For example, with expected power optimizations, such as decreased supply voltages and increases in memory

density, the number of DRAM errors is expected to increase for future exascale systems. To address these faults, current HPC systems typically include some form of Error Correction Code (ECC). The most common memory resilience scheme is the Single-symbol Error Correction and Double-symbol Error Detection (SEC-DED) [4]. The frequent ECC events will introduce overhead and performance degradation is unavoidable despite offering computation task [5]. Thus, performance degradation due to sub-health components inevitably leads to performance variability of numerical simulation applications.

In the presence of sub-health components and operating system interference, the processors or nodes with same architecture will export different performance during system runtime. The communication network topology and contention for shared network resources lead to the performance variability of data transfer between remote processes. From the above analysis, the performance variability in large scale high performance computer is the root cause of application performance variability.

### 1.3   The Impact of Performance Variability

For the Bulk Synchronous Parallel (BSP) applications in Fig. 1, in order to ensure load balance, all the tasks have the same computation, communication and memory access performance. All the tasks will reach the synchronization point (for example a global barrier) at the same time and the wait time should be as low as possible. With the scale of systems and numerical simulation program parallelism increases, the contention for shared resources, communication network topology, operating system interference and sub-health components will have a high probability and become common features in HPC systems. All of the common overheads will destroy the load balance in Fig. 1. Due to the overhead and synchronization, each computing phase is prolonged to the duration of the slowest task. The impact of performance variability overhead is illustrated in Fig. 2.

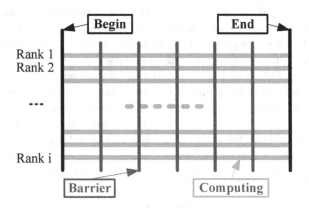

**Fig. 1.** BSP model

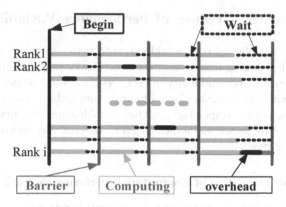

**Fig. 2.** Impact of performance variability overhead

Especially for the massively parallel, long running time and including frequent global synchronization activities HPC workload, the performance degradation of partial tasks will influence all the other tasks. So, toward massive parallelism, the performance variability of HPC systems would significantly reduce applications performance. Some research results argued the impact of performance variability from operating system noise. For example, by removing noise caused by several types of daemons, confining daemons to the cluster manager, and removing the cluster manager and the RMS cluster monitor from each cluster's compute pool, the performance of SAGE on ASCI Q system had been doubled [6]. Another example, by using kernel level noise injection, the OS noise has a dramatic impact on the performance of CTH, SAGE, POP three applications at scale [7]. In our study [8], we proposed one quantitative analysis method named FWQ-MPI which is used to analyze the impact of system noise based on computation and communication features from parallel applications. By FWQ-MPI method, we analyzed the impact of system noise on large-scale sparse linear algebraic equations in detailed. The quantitative results showed that the operating system noise reduce the performance of sparse linear algebra solver 30–70% for 1024, 2048, 4096 parallelism.

The performance variability of computing systems bas received attention for a long time. Back in 1994 and 1996, the researchers noticed the performance variability of point-to-point and All-to-All communications on IBM 9076 SP1 [9], SP2 [10] systems. In recent years, many groups have paid more attention to performance variability and variability towards tomorrow's exascale computing. Such as the HPC-Colony project [11] achieves high scalability through coordinated scheduling techniques and other strategies aimed at reducing the operating system overhead; from 2011 the international workshop on runtime and operating systems for supercomputers (ROSS) [12] selected "system noise analysis and prevention" as the main topic of discussion.

For different high performance computers and various numerical simulation applications, the root cause of system performance variability will be complex and various. The impact of every performance variability causes on numerical simulation applications will be diverse, so there are different ideas introduced in related researches. We summarize the key ideas and contributions of related researches and give a literature review about quantitative measurement of performance variability in HPC systems.

## 2  Quantitative Measurement of Performance Variability

The performance variability of HPC workloads reflects the instability of HPC systems performance, so the running time of relative benchmarks can be used to quantitative measurement of performance variability in HPC systems. Some related research works construct a sequence of benchmarks including computation, memory access and communication activities respectively. After establishing baselines of standard benchmarks, the Performance variability of HPC systems was tested via a series of benchmark running time.

### 2.1  Quantitative Evaluation of Computation Performance Variability

The Performance variability in computing components is primarily due to interference from operating system noise. Operating system noise as a cause of application performance degradation has been extensively studied via various techniques. In the HPC community, this problem was first demonstrated by Petrini et al. [6]: they explained how OS noise and other system activities dramatically impact the performance of a large cluster. The quantitative analysis methods of OS noise are applicable for the quantitative evaluation of Performance variability in computing components. The current benchmarks support three different quantitative analysis methods: Fixed Work Quantum (FWQ) [13, 14], Fixed Time Quantum (FTQ) [14, 15] and Selfish DeTour (SDT) [14].

#### 2.1.1  Fixed Work Quantum
The fixed work quantum benchmark performs a fixed amount of work multiple times and records the time it takes for each run. The overhead of OS noise is calculated based on the running time of FWQ benchmark. Figure 3 shows a schematic sketch. The fixed work quantum steps are introduced as follows:

First Step: construct a fixed amount of work named $W$;
Second Step: the $W$ is performed $n$ times and all the run time are $T[n]$;

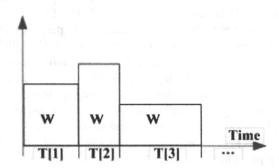

**Fig. 3.** Schematic sketch for fixed work quantum method [15]

Third Step: set $T_{min} = min\{T_1, T_2, \cdots, T_n\}$, $T_{min}$ is defined as the ideal running time of $W$ without system noise interference.

Fourth Step: the total amount of system noise is defined as follows,

$$N_{all} = \sum_{i=1}^{n} \{T[i] - T_{min}\} = \sum_{i=i}^{n} T[i] - n \times T_{min} \qquad (1)$$

The proportion of system noise to all time is defined:

$$P_{noise} = N_{all} \Big/ \sum_{i=i}^{n} T[i] = 1 - \left( n \times T_{min} \Big/ \sum_{i=1}^{n} T[i] \right) \qquad (2)$$

### 2.1.2 Fixed Time Quantum

The Fixed Time Quantum (FTQ) had been described in [15]: A very small work quantum is performed until a fixed time quantum has exceeded, for each iteration, it is recorded how many workload iterations were carried out. In the absence of noise this number should be equal for every sample. When there is noise this number varies. Because every sample takes an equal amount of time, periodicity in the occurrence of noise can be analyzed with this method. Figure 4 shows a schematic sketch. The fixed work quantum steps are introduced as follows:

First Step: construct a loop named $W$ and the amount of work in $W$ is defined as C;
Second Step: for every fixed time named T, the $W$ is performed and records the amount of work that was done. All the amount of work are $C[n]$;
Third Step: $C[n]$ is well-behaved in the way it samples and hence can be used for frequency- and time-domain analysis [15]. The analysis results give the key features of OS noise.

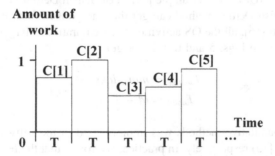

**Fig. 4.** Schematic sketch for fixed time quantum method [15]

### 2.1.3 Selfish Detour

"Selfish DeTour (SDT)" runs in a tight loop and measures the time for each iteration. The Code for Selfish Detour is shown in Fig. 5 [16].

```
count=0;
min_ticks=INFINITY;
current = rdtsc();
while(count<N) {
      prev=current;
      current=rdtsc();    /* keep the previous timer value */
      td=current-prev;    /*obtain the current timer value*/
      if(td>threshold) {/*If an iteration takes longer than the
                  threshold, then the timestamp  is recorded. */
            detour[count++]=prev;
            detour[count++]=current;
      }
      if(td<min_ticks) min_ticks=td;
}
```

**Fig. 5.** The code for Selfish Detour [16]

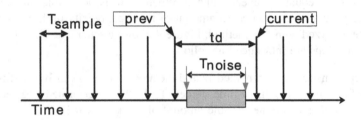

**Fig. 6.** The sample for Selfish Detour [16]

From the Fig. 5, Selfish DeTour method is same with Fixed Work Quantum when the amount of W is NULL, so the sample period of Selfish Detour is shorter than FWQ and FTQ. The Selfish Detour method can get the fine-grained features of OS noise, as shown in the Fig. 6 [16], all the OS activities whose duration is larger than $T_{sample}$ can be measured. From the Figs. 5 and 6, we can get:

$$T_{sample} = min\_ticks$$
$$T_{noise} = td - T_{sample}$$

$$(3)$$

These three quantitative methods was implemented in the software P-SNAP [13], Netgauge [17], ftq [15] respectively. In practice, we found that the features of OS noise in multicore and multicpu nodes are variable between different usage patterns. In order to measure the noise of all nodes in large scale systems, we implement a new tools called NoiseProfiler [8, 18] which include FWQ, FTQ and Selfish Detour and achieve three measuring processes named Full Node, Single CPU and Single Core, corresponding to three usage patterns of HPC systems.

## 2.2 Quantitative Evaluation of Memory Access Performance Variability

The memory access Performance variability might suffer from the deep memory hierarchies, shared cache contention in multicore chip and NUMA multiprocessors. There are no a formal and unified approach to the evaluation of Memory Access Performance variability. The quantitative evaluation benchmarks in related researches are derived from each numerical simulation applications respectively.

The research in [19] is the representative example. The contribution of [19] is the analysis of a novel source of system variability that is related to the OS services such as memory allocation management rather than the kernel itself. To solve the Scalability Challenges for Massively Parallel AMR Applications, three major methods that improved AMR scaling behavior has be applied: improving communication locality, converting to metadata management algorithms with O(N) computational complexity, and optimizing coarse-fine boundary value computations [19]. However the Runtime Variability is significantly higher. To help isolate scaling bottlenecks in the Chombo AMR infrastructure, the authors created and run benchmarks for an AMR hyperbolic gas dynamics computation to quantitative evaluation of Performance variability in four HPC systems, such as Jaguar/Catamount XT4, Jaguar/Catamount XT3, Jaguar/CNL XT4 and Franklin/CNL XT4. Figure 7 shows the runtime distributions of 8192 MPI process ranks for the AMR hyperbolic gas dynamics running on the evaluated systems. The representation in Fig. 7 shows a clear evidence in the Performance variability on Franklin/CNL XT4 and Jaguar/CNL XT4 (the runtime is 156–175 s), however the runtime on Jaguar/Catamount XT4 and Jaguar/Catamount XT3 has small variability. The investigation showed that the traditional concerns over load imbalance and communication volume were not as critical to application performance. The investigation also revealed that heap management of Compute Node Linux was an equally important source of performance variability. For quantitative evaluation of memory access Performance variability, the coefficient of variations (CoV) of PAPI_TLB_DM (Data translation look aside buffer misses), PAPI_L1_DCA (Level 1

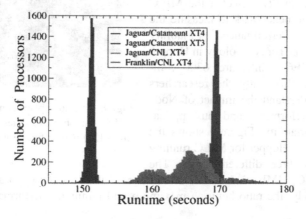

**Fig. 7.** Histogram of runtime variability for the AMR hyperbolic gas dynamics runs on the evaluated systems [19]

| Events | BArena | | BArena + env vars | | CArena | |
|---|---|---|---|---|---|---|
| | avg | CoV (%) | avg | CoV (%) | avg | CoV (%) |
| | | | secondslopediffsf. | | | |
| Time | 14 | 6.05 | 4 | 1.47 | 7 | 1.42 |
| PAPI_TLB_DM | 5,928,940 | 15.59 | 1,328,920 | 1.42 | 2,659,650 | 3.01 |
| PAPI_L1_DCA | 4,525,960,000 | 2.14 | 3,486,850,000 | 0.16 | 3,488,510,000 | 0.16 |
| PAPI_FP_OPS | 169 | 5.51 | 408 | 5.64 | 226 | 3.99 |
| DATA_CACHE_MISSES | 581,476,000 | 6.00 | 204,598,000 | 0.16 | 204,569,000 | 0.16 |

**Fig. 8.** CrayPat dump of Chombo AMR code performance [19]

data cache accesses), PAPI_FP_OPS (Floating point operations), DATA_CA-CHE_MISSES (Data Cache Misses) events as well as the times spent in functions can be selected. Figure 8 gives the evaluation results of Performance variability for three memory allocation system in CNL including Barena, BArena+env vars and Carena. For the function secondslopediffsf_, the performance variability with "BArena+env vars" memory allocation system decreased comparing against Barena and Carena.

Another study in [20] selected ten memory intensive benchmarks to quantitative assessment of memory access Performance variability. The variation in benchmarks' runtime and cache miss-rate was used to analyze the performance variability for next-touch, random and Round-robin memory allocation policies.

### 2.3 Quantitative Evaluation of Communication Performance Variability

The topology, contention for shared network resources and subhealth components are the root cause of communication Performance variability. Various types of communication intensive benchmarks are used to evaluate the communication Performance variability in HPC systems.

The research in [21] selected the MILC application as the benchmark to measure the communication Performance variability caused by Cray 3D Torus topology in Hopper system (Cray XE6 architecture, 6300 compute nodes). In this study the researchers proposed to understand the impact of Node Placement on performance and thus application runtime variability. Figure 9 shows the node placement in Hopper for MILC running on 8192 cores three different times. The

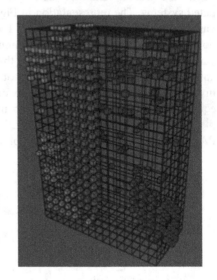

**Fig. 9.** The node placement in Hopper for MILC run on 8192 cores three different times [21] (Color figure online)

running (NERSC_TIME) time is 887.12 s (Blue), 1298.88 s (Orange) and 2462.33 s (Red) respectively; the ratio between maximum and minimum performance values is three times.

Another example in [22], the authors use pF3D, a highly scalable, communication heavy, parallel application to quantify performance reproducibility on three different parallel architectures: IBM Blue Gene/P, IBM Blue Gene/Q and Cray XE6. The Average Messaging Rates was used as the metric for evaluating Communication Performance variability. The Evaluation results show that the Node Placement and contention for shared network resources in CIELO and HOPPER system (Cray XE6 architecture) influence PF3D's performance: the communication time of PF3D varied from 36% faster to 69% slower when compared to the average. In [23], the Performance variability caused by contention in fat-tree topology is analyzed in detail.

## 3  Conclusions

From the above analysis, the quantitative evaluation methods of Performance variability in HPC systems can be summarized as follows: the synthesized benchmarks should be formed considering the characteristics from both numerical simulation applications and HPC systems, and the variations of runtime metrics from these benchmarks are selected to evaluate the Performance variability of HPC systems. Thus, the key question of benchmarks design is how to reflect the characteristics of HPC systems and numerical simulation applications accurately and comprehensively. In addition, the quantitative benchmarks of Performance variability also take into account the needs for root cause analysis and impact assessment.

## References

1. The Top 500 Supercomputer List. http://www.top500.org
2. Shalf, J., Dosanjh, S., Morrison, J.: Exascale computing technology challenges. In: Palma, J. M.L.M., Daydé, M., Marques, O., Lopes, J.C. (eds.) VECPAR 2010. LNCS, vol. 6449, pp. 1–25. Springer, Heidelberg (2011). doi:10.1007/978-3-642-19328-6_1
3. Benoit, A., Cavelan, A., Robert, Y., Sun, H.: Assessing general-purpose algorithms to cope with fail-stop and silent errors. (Research Report) RR-8599, INRIA (2014)
4. Hardy, D., Sideris, I., Ladas, N., Sazeides, Y.: Modelling the performance vulnerability of arrays to permanent faults. In: The 9th Workshop on Silicon Errors in Logic System Effects (2013)
5. Allan, B.: Memory reliability and performance degradation: hunting rabbits with an elephant gun. In: Monitoring and Analysis for High Performance Computing Systems Plus Applications (HPCMASPA) Workshop. IEEE Cluster (2014)
6. Petrini, F., Kerbyson, D.K., Pakin, S.: The case of the missing supercomputer performance: achieving optimal performance on the 8,192 processors of ASCI Q. In: 2003 ACM/IEEE Conference IEEE Supercomputing (2003)
7. Ferreira, K.B., Bridges, P., Brightwell, R.: Characterizing application sensitivity to OS interference using kernel-level noise injection. In: Proceedings of the 2008 ACM/IEEE Conference on Supercomputing, SC 2008, Piscataway, NJ, USA, pp. 1–12. IEEE Press (2008)
8. Wu, L., Wei, Y., Xu, X., Liu, X.: Impact of system noise by quantitative analysis. J. Comput. Res. Dev. **52**(5), 1146–1152 (2015)

9. Mraz, R.: Reducing the variance of point to point transfers in the IBM 9076 parallel computer. In: Proceedings of the 1994 ACM/IEEE Conference on Supercomputing. IEEE Computer Society Press (1994)
10. Tabe, T.B., Hardwick, J.P. Stout, Q.F.: Statistical analysis of communication time on the IBM SP2. Comput. Sci. Stat. 347–351 (1996)
11. HPC-Colony Project. http://www.hpc-colony.org/
12. International Workshop on Runtime and Operating System for Supercomputer. http://htor. inf.ethz.ch/ross2012/
13. Johnson, G.: P-SNAP: a system benchmark for quantifying operating system interference or noise. http://www.c3.lanl.gov/pal/software/psnap/
14. Hoefler, T., Schneider, T., Lumsdaine, A.: Characterizing the influence of system noise on large-scale applications by simulation. In: Proceedings of the 2010 ACM/IEEE International Conference for High Performance Computing, Networking, Storage and Analysis. IEEE Computer Society, pp. 1–11 (2010)
15. Sottile, M., Minnich, R.: Analysis of microbenchmarks for performance tuning of clusters. In: 2004 IEEE International Conference on IEEE Cluster Computing, pp. 371–377 (2004)
16. Beckman, P., Iskra, K., Yoshii, K., et al.: Benchmarking the effects of operating system interference on extreme-scale parallel machines. Cluster Comput. 11(1), 3–16 (2008)
17. Hoefler, T., Mehlan, T., Lumsdaine, A., Rehm, W.: Netgauge: a network performance measurement framework. In: Perrott, R., Chapman, B.M., Subhlok, J., de Mello, R.F., Yang, Laurence T. (eds.) HPCC 2007. LNCS, vol. 4782, pp. 659–671. Springer, Heidelberg (2007). doi:10.1007/978-3-540-75444-2_62
18. Wu, L., Wei, Y., Liu, X.: The quantitative measurement of system noise in multicore multiprocessor clustered systems. In: CCF HPC CHINA, Zhangjiajie, Hunan Province (2012)
19. Van Straalen, B., Shalf, J., Ligocki, T., et al.: Scalability challenges for massively parallel AMR applications. In: IEEE International Symposium on Parallel and Distributed Processing, IPDPS 2009. IEEE, pp. 1–12 (2009)
20. Pusukuri, K.K., Gupta, R., Bhuyan, L.N.: Thread Tranquilizer: dynamically reducing performance variation. ACM Trans. Archit. Code Optim. (TACO) 8(4), 46 (2012)
21. Application performance variability on hopper. http://www.nersc.gov/users/computational-systems/hopper/performance-and-optimization/application-performance-variability-on-hopper/
22. Bhatele, A., et al.: There goes the neighborhood: performance degradation due to nearby jobs. In: Proceedings of SC13: International Conference for High Performance Computing, Networking, Storage and Analysis. ACM (2013)
23. Jokanovic, A., et al.: Impact of inter-application contention in current and future HPC systems. In: 2010 IEEE 18th Annual Symposium on High Performance Interconnects (HOTI). IEEE (2010). Author, F.: Article title. Journal 2(5), 99–110 (2016)

# GDCRT: In-Memory 2D Geographical Dynamic Cascading Range Tree

Yinxing Hou[1,2](✉), Haixia Wang[1], and Dongsheng Wang[1]

[1] Tsinghua National Laboratory for Information Science and Technology,
Tsinghua University, Beijing 100084, China
houyx16@mails.tsinghua.edu.cn, {hx-wang,wds}@mail.tsinghua.edu.cn
[2] Department of Computer Science and Technology, Tsinghua University,
Beijing 100084, China

**Abstract.** With the rapid increase of GPS users, the performance of location-based services (LBS) has gradually become a hot research topic. As the core algorithm of LBS, fast range query processing with massive data become the key problem. Till now, the main structures in this field are R-tree and its varieties. Although they can be adapted to a variety of dynamical data-set, and process insert/deletion in $O(\log n)$, there are still two essential defects when processing range query in it. Firstly, their time boundary for range query is $O(\sqrt{n})$. Secondly, their performance are based on heuristic algorithm. Given these two facts, the performance of R-trees is intolerable and unstable. Thus, in this paper, we introduce Geographical Dynamic Cascading Range Tree (GDCRT), a 2D dynamic index tree aiming at geographical range query in points data-set. The main innovation of GDCRT is to make fractional cascaded Range-tree dynamical by applying AVL-tree's balance principle. For insertion and deletion, its time complexity is $O(\log n)$, which is equal to R-tree. For range query, its time boundary is $\theta(k + \log n)$, which is lower compared to R-tree series. And final experiment results also prove the correctness and efficiency of our structure.

**Keywords:** Geographical index · 2D dynamic tree · Location-based services (LBS) · Fast range query · High-performance indexing

## 1  Introduction

As is known, the information needed in human daily life has strong geographical locality. Currently, with the mature of the location system, location based services are widely utilized. Smart phone users use LBS to search for friends, shops, attractions nearby. This refers to range query in data structure field, which request all points in an given area (such as a rectangle). As GPS users increase, both the data-set and the frequency of range query grow. Without effective indexing method, query operations often become performance bottlenecks.

© Springer International Publishing AG 2017
Y. Dou et al. (Eds.): APPT 2017, LNCS 10561, pp. 87–98, 2017.
DOI: 10.1007/978-3-319-67952-5_8

To address these need, we have investigated the existing data structures. R-tree families meet the expectation for the cost of insertion and deletion. In industry they are hired in many database such as Microsoft SQL server [6]. But their performance depends on an heuristic space segmentation algorithm, which is unreliable. More importantly, as R-tree is not optimized for range query, the range query's time complexity is as slow as $O(\sqrt{n})$. Grid structures and space-filling curves is dynamical and process searching as fast as hash table. However, they need to be adapted to R-tree as they can't support range query naturally.

Generally, we found that though there are structures with similar interface, in terms of efficient range query, none of those is satisfactory. Meanwhile, all the technology mentioned above directly organized data in disk. Even though data can be well paged, the bandwidth of the disk is still the bottleneck of the algorithm. Considering the exponential growth of memory size and decline in its price over the past decades [13], we believe that virtual memory and paging technology are no more necessary for meta-data indexing. Storing all tree nodes in memory allows us organize data flexibly rather than page everything.

Therefore, for the requirements summed above, we propose Geographical Dynamic Cascading Range Tree (GDCRT), a new structure whose the time cost is $O(log(n))$ for all operations. The main contribution of the paper includes:

1. Propose the concept of in-memory meta-data index tree for large data-set.
2. Modify 2D range tree to support dynamic updates with $O(\log n)$ time cost using AVL balance strategy.
3. By adapting fractional cascading to the 2D AVL-tree, we accelerate the range query process from $O(\log^2 n + k)$ level to $O(\log n + k)$.
4. We verify the time complexity of GDCRT in practice by implementing GDCRT in Redis.

The next sections arranged as follows. Section 2 focuses on the background knowledge for a better understanding. Section 3 gives the definition of GDCRT as well as the algorithm for update and range query. The time complexity of GDCRT will be analyzed theoretically in Sect. 4. And Sect. 5 writes experimental data as an evidence of the complexity analysis. In Sect. 6, related works are listed. Section 7 draws a conclusion to our work.

## 2      Background

Since GDCRT is based on the three algorithms of AVL tree, range tree, and fractional cascading, it is necessary to briefly describe their principles in this section. So that the algorithms can be defined more clearly.

### 2.1      Range Tree

Range tree [3] is a static multi-dimensional space search tree designed aiming at range queries. We draw lessons from its two-dimension situation. Before we introduce the principle of it, the definition of range query is needed for a better understanding:

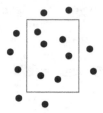

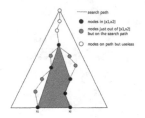

**Fig. 1.** Typical range query example    **Fig. 2.** Range query in range tree

For a bounded point set $S = \{p_1, p_2, \ldots, p_{n-1}, p_n\}$ in two-dimension space $V = [x_{min}, x_{max}] * [y_{min}, y_{max}]$, a range query requires the subset $S'$ represents all the points located in the given rectangle $V = [x_{left}, x_{right}] * [y_{bottom}, y_{top}]$ (see Fig. 1).

The main difficulty of this operation is how to avoid meaningless access to the points whose $x \in [x_1, x_2]$ but $y \notin [y_1, y_2]$. Range tree manages to solve this by the thought described below:

Build a $xTree$ for $x$ values, on every node $xNode_i$ of $xTree$, build a $yTree$ which contains all the $y$ value of the nodes in $xNode_i$'s subtree. Therefore, a range tree is processed as Fig. 2 shows:

1. For the range $[x_1, x_2] * [y_1, y_2]$, we look for the boundary values $x_1$ and $x_2$ in the $xTree$ and mark the path as $Path_{x1}$ and $Path_{x2}$.
2. We access all the nodes on the shadow border (black nodes), add them to results if their y coordinates are in $[y_1, y_2]$.
3. Apparently, for the shadow-side child $xNode_{sc}$ of each border node, all its sub-trees satisfy $x \in [x_1, x_2]$ (shaded portion). Hence, directly searching $yTree_{sc}$ of those $xNode_{sc}$ will get the results. This avoids visiting the inner part of the shadow and makes the process fast.

The time cost of this algorithm is $O(k + \log n)$, where k is size of result set, and $\log n$ is the length of two paths.

## 2.2 AVL Tree

AVL tree [7] is a basic linear balance tree. For every tree node, AVL demands its left and right sub-trees satisfy $|height_{left} - height_{right}| \leq 1$. GDCRT use 3-4 reconnection to ensure this condition.

As Fig. 3 displays, the gray subtree makes the height of node $p = (h + 2)$, resulting in imbalance of g ($|(h + 2) - h| \geq 1$). To re-balance g, we only need to adjust the vertical relationship among g, v, p, which we call 3-4 reconnection.

## 2.3 Fractional Cascading

Fractional cascading [10] is an optimization technique for range search in sub-set. Given an sorted number set $S = \{a_1 \ldots a_i \ldots a_n\}$ and its subset $S_1 = \{b_1 \ldots b_i \ldots b_n\}$, fractional cascading records a map M defined as below:

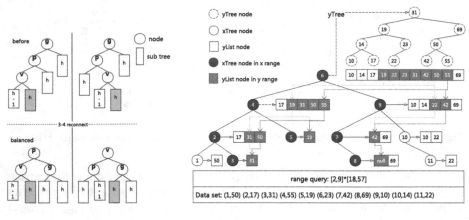

**Fig. 3.** 3-4 reconnection      **Fig. 4.** Range query in GDCRT (Color figure online)

$$M^g(a_i) = b_j \text{ where } b_{j-1} \le a_i \le b_j \tag{1}$$

$$M^l(a_i) = b_k \text{ where } b_k \le a_i \le b_{k+1} \tag{2}$$

Thus, for a range query whose result in $S$ is $[a_i, a_j]$ $a_i, a_j \in S$, we can write its result in $S_1$ as $[M^g(a_i), M^l(a_j)]$. The time consumption is $O(1)$ while directly recalculation in $S_1$ is $O(n)$.

# 3    Geographical Dynamic Cascading Range Tree

In this section, we denote the definition of GDCRT, including a brief illustration of a range query on GDCRT. Then, we explain the main steps of update on GDCRT, followed by a detailed algorithm. At last, we organize the illustrated range query process into a precise algorithm.

## 3.1    Structure

Firstly, we give a brief illustration in Fig. 4. In the figure, we organize 11 points in GDCRT, and process an range query over this GDCRT. For range query, we first find eligible $yNodes$ in $yTree$ (19 to 55). Then as we processing search in $xTree$, the $M^g$ and $M^l$ are passed to every visited node (the green dotted line for $M^g$ and red for $M^l$). Therefore, given a $xNode$, we can directly answer which points in its $yList$ is in range. Hence, when we finish searching $xTree$, we get the result without checking every eligible $xNode$ if its y coordinate is in range. In Fig. 4 the result set should be: (3, 31); (4, 55); (5, 19); (6, 23); (7, 42).

The detailed definition goes as follow:

We define the height of a tree node as the number of nodes on the path from itself to its the farthest descendants (including itself and the farthest descendants). For point set $S = \{p_1, p_2, \ldots, p_{n-1}, p_n\}$, in which $p_i$ is represented as $(x_i, y_i)$, we record it by:

1. Store x coordinate using AVL-tree [7] as $xTree$.
2. Store all points' y coordinate in the root of $xTree$ ($xRoot$) using AVL-tree as $yTree$.
3. In every $xNode_i$ except $xRoot$, build a ordered list marked as $yList_i$, which contains the y coordinate of the points whose x coordinate is in the descendants of $xNode_i$ ($subTree_i$).
4. For every Internal $yList_i$, given the left child of $xNode_i$ as $xNode_{lc}$, and the other as $xNode_{rc}$. Do:
   (a) As $yList_{lc}$ is subset of $yList_i$, for every $yList_i$ element, we record the fractional cascading map value from it to the $yList_{lc}$ (see formulas 1 and 2). We call these $M_{lc}^g(y_k)$ and $M_{lc}^l(y_k)$, where $y_k$ is the y value of $yList_i$ elements.
   (b) Repeat step (a) replacing $yList_{lc}$ with $yList_{rc}$ and call the map member as $M_{rc}^g(y_k)$ and $M_{rc}^l(y_k)$.
5. Consider $yTree$ as a $yList$, apply step 4 on it.

### 3.2  Insertion

Using AVL strategy, insertion of GDCRT contains three main operations:

1. Insert in $xTree$ and $yTree$, which is as simple as AVL tree.
2. Maintain $yList$ while inserting.
3. Correct $yList$ after 3-4 Reconnection.

**Maintaining Y List While Inserting.** To insert a new point ($foo$) into the GDCRT, we first insert $foo.x$ in $xTree$ and $foo.y$ in $yTree$. Then, we must insert $foo.y$ in every $yList_i$ that $xNode_i$ is on the path between $xRoot$ and $xNode_{foo}$. But as Fig. 5 displays, problem remains when we insert $foo.y$ in the $yList$ of $xNode_i$'s child:

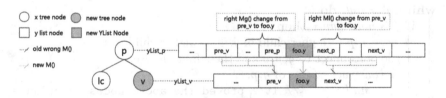

**Fig. 5.** Insertion in y list (Color figure online)

Assuming $foo.y$ has already been inserted in $yList_i$. Before $yList_v$ changes, the $M_{rc}^l(y_k)$ of the nodes from $next_p$ to $next_v$ is $pre_v$ (red line). After $foo.y$ was insert $yList_v$, we need to change these record to foo.y (the green line). Same correction need to be applied to $M_{rc}^g(y_k)$. A simple algorithm is denoted as below to do this:

---

**Algorithm 1.** Adjustment after Inserting $foo.y$ in $yList_p$

---

1. $xNode_p \leftarrow Parent(xNode_v)$ and mark every variable as Fig. 5 shows;
2. $j \leftarrow pre_p$;
3. **while** $j$ is not $next_v$ and not NULL **do**
4.    | $j \leftarrow j.next$;
5.    | $M_{now}^l(j) \leftarrow (foo.y$ in $yList_v)$;      // $now := (is\_v\_left\_child)?lc : rc$
6. **end**
7. **from** $next_p$ **to** $pre_v$ in $yList_p$, do same to $M_{now}^g(j)$;

---

**Correcting Y List After 3-4 Reconnection.** Take Fig. 3 as example, after 3-4 Reconnection, sub-tree of node g, v, p changes dramatically, which means the information in g, v, p's $yList$ would be wrong. Because too many nodes in their sub-tree has changed. The only viable solution is to reconstruct the three $yList$.

To implement the solution, we first reconstruct $yList_g$ by merging the $yList$ of its two children. Then do so to its bother and parent (p and v). One should notice that both $yLists$ and the $M(y)$ maps between them need to be corrected.

This operation has some side effect on the time complexity. Fortunately, We can prove that all operations are still $log(n)$ time consuming. This part is detailed in Sect. 4.2.

**Detailed Insert Algorithm.** Combining all three operations above, we here provide the detailed algorithm for insertion. Assuming that point $foo = (foo.x, foo.y)$ will be inserted into the GDCRT, we need to do the following:

---

**Algorithm 2.** Insertion of GDCRT

---

1. in $xTree$, find $foo$'s parent, mark as $XNode_{hot}$;
2. insert $xNode_{foo}$ as a child of $xNode_{hot}$;      // Insert in $xTree$
3. $j \leftarrow xNode_{hot}$;
4. **while** $j! = null$ **do**
5.    | **if** $j$ is not balance **then**
6.    |    | $g \leftarrow j$, $p \leftarrow$ higher child of $j$, $v \leftarrow$ higher child of $p$;
7.    |    | do 3-4connect to $g, p, v$ and their four children;
8.    |    | reconstruct $yLists$ of $g, p, v$;
9.    |    | $j \leftarrow null$ ;      // It's proved the above nodes is balance
10.    | **end**
11.    | $j \leftarrow j$'s parent;
12. **end**
13. $j \leftarrow xNode_{foo}$ ;      // Insert in $yLists$
14. **while** $j! = xRoot$ **do**
15.    | Insert $foo.y$ in the $yList_j$;
16.    | $rc \leftarrow j$, process Algorithm 1 on $j$ and its parent;
17.    | $j \leftarrow j$'s parent;
18. **end**
19. Insert $foo.y$ in $yTree$;      // Insert in $yTree$

---

We especially emphasize that $yTree$ can be considered as a special $yList$ to fit Algorithm 1. This is feasible in practice.

## 3.3 Deletion

The deletion is inverse operation of insertion, which is similar to insertion in principle, except that the order of operations is opposite to insertion. That means the data should be firstly deleted in $yTree$, then in $yLists$, as last in $xTree$. For people who implement GDCRT, they should notice that if two $xNodes$ need to be swapped, the $yLists$ between them should also be corrected using Algorithm 1.

## 3.4 Range Query on GDCRT

The Fig. 4 has illustrated the process of range query on GDCRT. Here we give a precise algorithm for it. Supposing we want to find which points locate in range $R = [x_1, x_2] * [y_1, y_2]$:

---
**Algorithm 3.** Range query in GDCRT

---
1. search $x_1$ in $xTree$, mark the path as $P_1$, the end node as $xNode_1$;
2. search $x_2$ in $xTree$, mark the path as $P_2$, the end node as $xNode_2$;
3. $xNode_{sp} \leftarrow$ the node where $P_1$ and $P_2$ separate;
4. search $y_1$ or its next in $yTree$, the end node as $y_{lower}$(lower bound);
5. search $y_2$ or its previous in $yTree$, the end node as $y_{upper}$(upper bound);
6. **foreach** $j$ on $P_1$ **from** $xRoot$ to $xNode_{sp}$ **do**
7.      $y_{lower} \leftarrow M^g_{now}(y_{lower})$;
8.      $y_{upper} \leftarrow M^l_{now}(y_{upper})$ ;             // $now := (is\_j\_left\_child)?lc : rc$
9. **end**
10. $y'_{lower} \leftarrow y_{lower}$, $y'_{upper} \leftarrow y_{upper}$;
11. **foreach** $j$ on $P_1$ **from** $xNode_{sp}$ to $xNode_1$ **do**
12.      $y'_{lower} \leftarrow M^g_{now}(y'_{lower})$, $y'_{upper} \leftarrow M^l_{now}(y'_{upper})$;
13.      **if** $j.x$ in $[x_1, x_2]$ **then**
14.          **output** $j$ **if** $j.y$ in $[y_1, y_2]$;
15.          $y'_l \leftarrow M^g_{rc}(y'_{lower})$, $y'_u \leftarrow M^l_{rc}(y'_{upper})$;
16.          **output** nodes **from** $y'_l$ to $y'_u$ in the $yList$ of $j$'s shadow-side child.
17.      **end**
18. **end**
19. **from** $xNode_{sp}$ to $xNode_2$ on $P_2$ repeat line 10 to 18.

---

## 4 Time Complexity

### 4.1 Range Query

To figure out the time complexity of range query, we directly count the nodes Algorithm 3 visits.

Firstly, nodes on $P_1$ and $P_2$ are visits, which is $\theta(\log n)$. Then, every node visited is in the result set. Assuming the result set size is $k$, the worst case time boundary of range query is $\theta(\log(n) + k)$.

## 4.2 Update

**Maintaining Y List While Inserting.** As Algorithm 1 displays (in Sect. 3.2), to insert a node in $xNode_v$'s $yList_v$, we need to access the nodes from $pre_v$ to $next_v$ in its parent's $ylist_p$ (see Fig. 5). The number of these nodes (mark as $N$) represents the time boundary (Mark as $Time_{yList}$) of Algorithm 1. These nodes are mainly from $xNode_{lc}$, which is bother of $xNode_v$. Thus, we calculate $N$ by converting it to the following problem:

Given an interval $I = [y_1, y_2]$ $y_1, y_2 \in \mathbf{R}$, we generate sorted set $m_1 = \{a_1, \ldots, a_n\}$, $m_2 = \{b_1, \ldots, b_n\}$ by randomly selecting n elements from $I$. Set $m = m_1 \cup m_2$. Now the number of accessed nodes is converted to the number of $b_j$ between $a_i$ and $a_{i+1}$ in $m$.

As Fig. 6 shows, the expectation of $\frac{L_{a_i - a_{i+1}}}{L_{y_2 - y_1}} = \frac{1}{n+1}$. So the $N$'s expectation is $Size(m_2) * \frac{L_{a_2 - a_1}}{L_{y_2 - y_1}} = \frac{n}{n+1} \leq 1$. Therefore, the expectation of $Time_{yList} = O(1)$. Hence, the time complexity of a naive update without 3-4 reconnection is:

$$Time_{yTree} + Time_{xTree} * Time_{yList} = O(\log n + \log(n) * 1) = O(\log n) \quad (3)$$

where $Time_{yTree}$ and $Time_{xTree}$ are the nodes accessed in AVL trees while updating (proved in [7]).

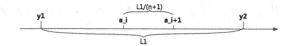

**Fig. 6.** Length from $a_i$ to $a_{i+1}$

**3-4 Reconnection.** When a 3-4 reconnection happens to nodes $g, p, v$, all the nodes in their $yList$ are visited, which is slow. Fortunately, not every update results in 3-4 reconnection. Actually, if we define $depth_k$ as the number of nodes between $Node_k$ and $Root$, we have the lemma below:

**Lemma 1.** *For n continuous updates, the nodes depth $= i$ suffers up to $2^i$ times 3-4 reconnection* [8,12].

Using this lemma, the time complexity of 3-4 reconnection for every single update is:

$$O(\frac{1}{n} * \sum_{i=1}^{\log n} 2^i * \frac{n}{2^i}) = O(\log n) \quad (4)$$

The updates complexity is the sum of naive update complexity and 3-4 reconnection complexity, which is $O(\log n)$.

# 5    Evaluation

In this section, we provide details on a set of experiments to evaluate the performance of GDCRT. Using C++ language, we implement GDCRT on a Linux server. The server has 32 GB memory. And we run a Redis [14] memory storage on it. We store all our tree nodes in Redis instead of directly in program. This may cause some loss in performance but make our code an understandable example of implementation. Because Redis uses some cache and pipeline strategy, the time cost result may be interfered and confusing. Here we assume that every Redis operation (read/write) is equal time consumption, then use the frequency of the storage operations to represent the time consumption level of an insertion/deletion. For example, the first insertion in an empty tree may need 1 write and 0 read.

**Update Performance.** At first, we test the time of updating single node in trees whose size range from 0 to 1500. To ensure the accuracy, we repeat the experiment 100 times. The results are displayed in Fig. 7(a).

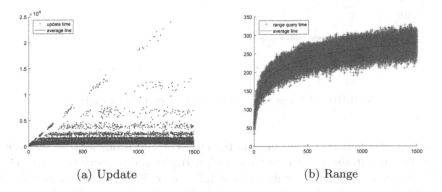

(a) Update                         (b) Range

**Fig. 7.** 1500 * 100 points performance (Color figure online)

As Fig. 7(a) displays, few points on the diagonal prove that only several 3-4 re-connections happen at the tree root during 150000 times updates. From the diagonal to the x-axis, points increase exponentially. This can be an evidence of Lemma 1. Moreover, after calculating the average performance of 100 times on each point (the blue line), we notice 99% nodes are around the average line. We use $y = a + b * \log x$ to fit the average data, the result is satisfactory as Fig. 8 shows. The R-square of all fitting is over 97%, which is enough high to prove that our experiment is an $O(\log n)$ process.

**Range Query Performance.** We range the tree size from 0 to 1500, and test the range query whose result set contains 1–20 elements. The results are displayed in Fig. 7(b), and the fitting result is also shown in Fig. 8. Compared to

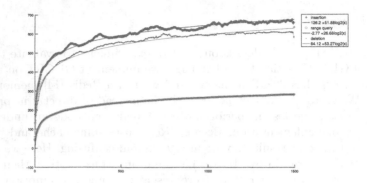

**Fig. 8.** Logarithmic fitting of the 1500 * 100 points performance (Color figure online)

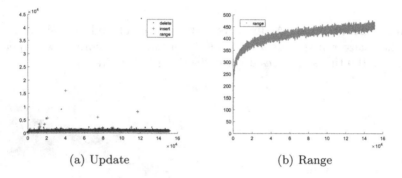

(a) Update                              (b) Range

**Fig. 9.** 100000 * 3 points performance (Color figure online)

update, range query cost less time and the time consumption variance is smaller. The fitting result also proves the time complexity of range query is $(\log n)$ level. To further verify the complexity of GDCRT, we build a 100000-nodes tree for several times and test the performance of it. The data shown in Fig. 9 meets the logarithm trends of the early test.

To conclude, we found that in practice, the time complexity of all operations on GDCRT is $O(\log n)$ level, which is as we expected. For update, few operations influencing the root node will cause performance degradation. But most of updates are fast. Averagely, updates are accomplished in $O(\log n)$. For range query, all operations can be finished in $O(\log n)$.

## 6    Related Work

High-performance spatial range query has long been a goal of the data structure. However, there is still no technology aiming at 2D geographical points case. As we have researched, the related technology can be classified into: (i) tree-based structure [1], (ii) grid structures [11], and (iii) space-filling curves [2,4]. Quad-tree is one of the most ordinary tree-based choices. It simply divides a square into four sub-squares recursively until every sub-square has few points. But with no balance strategy, it acts as a linked list on numerous data, and averagely 2–3 times slower compared to R-tree [9]. The principle of grid structures and space-filling curves are similar to Quad-tree, but they give every sub-square a uniquely identified string code. The string code has a beforehand protocol on code pattern. Hence, by converting coordinate to the patterned string code, sub-squares can be accessed like key-value pairs in hash table, which is fast. However, two problem remains in this program. On the one hand, if the sub-squares are too large, too many points contained in a single sub-square results in the low performance when searching in it. On the other hand, if the sub-squares are too small, a range query may overfill several sub-squares, the algorithm become chaotic. In practice, it is difficult to find a suitable size of division.

The R-tree uses a heuristic algorithm to partition the space into recursive bounding boxes, then builds B-tree based on these partitions. Due to the different choice of heuristic algorithm, R-tree families adapt themselves into various of use-cases, such as different partition shapes, lazy updates on frequently moving objects, fast bounding box on irregular objects, etc. However, speaking of range query on point set, R-tree is still unsatisfactory compared to GDCRT.

By combining R-tree and space-filling curves, hierarchical structure was introduced as an optimization. Currently it is used in structures such as Spatial-Hadoop [5] and E-tree [15]. It divides spatial data into two levels. Spatial data is first split using space-filling curves, then $R^+$-Tree is built in every sub-square. This optimization improves the performance of small range query that does not overfill the sub-square. But as this hierarchical structure can be transplanted into every index tree, the essential range query function are still relatively slow.

# 7  Conclusion and Future Work

**Conclusion.** In this paper, we have implemented a dynamical balanced index structure designed for 2-D range search. The structure is extraordinary for range query, and support update with relatively low complexity. As memory grows, GDCRT is supposed to index meta-data and layout in memory to offer the best performance. Although GDCRT is designed to index spatial date, it is also suitable for accessing data according to a composite key in database.

**Future Work.** Two future work remains: As discussed in Sect. 3.2, a total of $O(\log n)$ $yLists$ need to be fixed (Algorithm 1) for a single insertion/deletion. Considering $yLists$ are independent if their $xNodes$ are not connected, the $O(\log n)$ times Algorithm 1 can be parallelized. Also, adapting GDCRT into heuristic algorithm to fit distributed Systems is another work to be studied.

**Acknowledgments.** This work is supported by the National Key R&D Plan of China (Grant No. 2016YFB1000303); NSF of China (Grant No. 61373025); the National 863 High-Tech Program of China (Grant No. 2012AA010905).

# References

1. Balasubramanian, L., Sugumaran, M.: A state-of-art in R-tree variants for spatial indexing. Int. J. Comput. Appl. **42**(20), 35–41 (2012)
2. Balkić, Z., Šoštarić, D., Horvat, G.: GeoHash and UUID identifier for multi-agent systems. In: Jezic, G., Kusek, M., Nguyen, N.-T., Howlett, R.J., Jain, L.C. (eds.) KES-AMSTA 2012. LNCS, vol. 7327, pp. 290–298. Springer, Heidelberg (2012). doi:10.1007/978-3-642-30947-2_33
3. Bentley, J.L.: Multidimensional divide-and-conquer. Commun. ACM **23**(4), 214–229 (1980)
4. Chen, L., Cong, G., Jensen, C.S., Wu, D.: Spatial keyword query processing: an experimental evaluation. In: Proceedings of the VLDB Endowment, vol. 6, pp. 217–228. VLDB Endowment (2013)
5. Eldawy, A.: SpatialHadoop: towards flexible and scalable spatial processing using mapreduce. In: Proceedings of the 2014 SIGMOD Ph.D. Symposium, pp. 46–50. ACM (2014)
6. Fang, Y., Friedman, M., Nair, G., Rys, M., Schmid, A.E.: Spatial indexing in microsoft SQL server 2008. In: Proceedings of the 2008 ACM SIGMOD International Conference on Management of Data, pp. 1207–1216. ACM (2008)
7. Foster, C.C.: A generalization of AVL trees. Commun. ACM **16**(8), 513–517 (1973)
8. Fredman, M.L.: A lower bound on the complexity of orthogonal range queries. J. ACM (JACM) **28**(4), 696–705 (1981)
9. Kothuri, R.K.V., Ravada, S., Abugov, D.: Quadtree and R-tree indexes in oracle spatial: a comparison using GIS data. In: Proceedings of the 2002 ACM SIGMOD International Conference on Management of Data, pp. 546–557. ACM (2002)
10. Preparata, F.P., Shamos, M.: Computational Geometry: An Introduction. Springer Science & Business Media, Heidelberg (2012). doi:10.1007/978-1-4612-1098-6
11. Tropf, H., Herzog, H.: Multidimensional range search in dynamically balanced trees. Angew. Inf. **2**, 71–77 (1981)
12. Willard, D.E., Lueker, G.S.: Adding range restriction capability to dynamic data structures. J. ACM (JACM) **32**(3), 597–617 (1985)
13. Woo, S.: Dram and memory system trends (2004)
14. Zawodny, J.: Redis: lightweight key/value store that goes the extra mile. Linux Mag., **79** (2009)
15. Zhang, P., Zhou, C., Wang, P., Gao, B.J., Zhu, X., Guo, L.: E-tree: an efficient indexing structure for ensemble models on data streams. IEEE Trans. Knowl. Data Eng. **27**(2), 461–474 (2015)

# Eleven Code: A 3-Erasure MDS Code with Optimize Partial Stripes Writes

Hongwei Zhang[1,2,3], Jinsong Wang[1,2,3(✉)], and Sheng Lin[1,2,3]

[1] Tianjin University of Technology, Tianjin, China
jswang@tjut.edu.cn
[2] Tianjin Key Laboratory of Intelligence Computing and Novel Software Technology, Tianjin, China
[3] National Engineering Laboratory for Computer Virus Prevention and Control Technology, Tianjin, China

**Abstract.** In this paper, a novel 3-erasure code having advantages of both horizontal and vertical codes is described. Because of its parity construction liking the Greek Numeral XI, so we call it Eleven code. It is an MDS code expanded from H-code (an MDS code to optimal partial stripe writes in RAID-6) thus it has optimal storage property. To prove the accuracy of this new code's construction, a program also be designed in this paper; We compare Eleven code to Star code and T-code, and it shows that Eleven code reduces partial stripe write cost by up to 18.13% and 14.11%, respectively.

**Keywords:** 3-erasure code · MDS code · Partial stripe write · Performance evaluation

## 1 Introduction

With the progress of the society and the development of large data, the growing data information, the requirement of high stability and high availability has brought new opportunities and challenges in the field of storage technology. In large-scale data storage systems, multi-erasure codes have always been an efficient technology for its high storage performance and high reliability [1, 3]. As a scheme of a storage system, an m-erasure code uses m parity disks to encode its content on n data disks in order that the system can solve any m disk failures [2–5].

MDS (Maximum distance separable) codes [1, 6, 7] are one class of codes which offer data recovery against disk failures with the best storage structure of redundancy on multi-erasure coding technologies. In other words, MDS codes have optimal storage efficiency, which also be called optimal full stripe write complexity [9]. On the other hand, the complexity of a single write and partial stripe writes is also important in storage system [8, 10]. Partial stripe write is not like full stripe write which refers to the operation to write or update new data to each disks and do not care there have been data in them or not, it just focus on a part of disk in the array under writing. With increasing different read-write demand under processing information in disks, besides, in order to ensure the continuous availability of entire storage system by solving unbalanced I/O

Y. Dou et al. (Eds.): APPT 2017, LNCS 10561, pp. 99–104, 2017.
DOI: 10.1007/978-3-319-67952-5_9

distribution, the disk controller needs some efficient coding techniques, which can tolerate failures as well as have optimal partial stripe write performance, to execute I/O operations [2, 8].

In this paper, 3-erasure codes are considered and we categorize MDS codes into horizontal codes and vertical codes. Horizontal codes contain disks which only store data or parity information, in contrast, there are both data and parity packets stored within a single disk in vertical codes' disks [1, 8, 9]. In case of double fault tolerance, there are various kinds of codes either horizontal codes or vertical codes [13]. For the reasons of performance as well as disk I/O balance, we focus on the following properties with these codes, which we call them the efficiency properties:

1. *It has optimal performance in partial stripe writes.*
2. *It has Balanced I/O operation.*
3. *It has low single write complexity.*

As horizontal codes, EVENODD [11], RDP [10] and some other 2-erasure codes have been generalized to 3-erasure even m-erasure (m > 3) and besides, 2-erasure vertical codes such as B-code has further been generalized to m-erasure. However, the code satisfying the whole efficiency properties above like H-code has not been generalized by now. Accordingly, a 3-erasure code satisfied those properties from H-code is constructed in this paper, named Eleven code, which is similar to Greek numeral XI.

An outline of this paper is as follows. Section 2 briefly overviews the basis of this paper, namely, H-code reviews. The design of Eleven code is described in detail in Sect. 3.

## 2 H-Code Review

### 2.1 H-Code and Encoding

H-code is a hybrid MDS code scheme in RAID-6 which takes advantages of both vertical and horizontal codes [9]. In H-code, there are n disk (where $n = p + 1$, p is a prime number and $p \geq 5$), in the form of an array which is a $(p - 1) \times (p + 1)$ matrix, contains $(p - 1) \times (p + 1)$ elements, including p is a prime number. In the matrix, there are three elements: the data element, level calibration elements and the diagonal parity elements. A $C_{i,j}$ represents the i-th row first j column elements, the array of 0 is data elements to all elements, the last column is used to store all level calibration elements, the rest of the columns are also contains data elements and the diagonal elements of check. Specific coding formulas are given as follows:

Horizontal parity:

$$C_{i,p} = \sum_{j=0}^{p-1} C_{i,j}(j \neq i + 1) \tag{1}$$

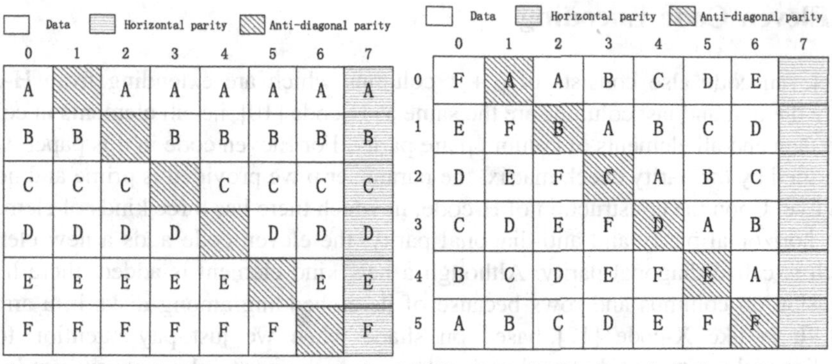

(a) The corresponding data elements in the same row calculate a horizontal element by XOR operations. For example, $C_{1,7}=C_{1,0} \oplus C_{1,1} \oplus C_{1,3} \oplus C_{1,4} \oplus C_{1,5} \oplus C_{1,6}$

(b) The corresponding data elements in all columns except its column and column p calculate a anti-diagonal element by XOR operations. For example, $C0_{,1}=C_{5,0} \oplus C_{0,2} \oplus C_{1,3} \oplus C_{2,4} \oplus C_{3,5} \oplus C_{4,6}$

**Fig. 1.** H-code with p = 7.

Anti-diagonal parity:

$$C_{i,i+1} = \sum_{j=0}^{p-1} C_{<p-2-i+j>_p,j} \ (j \neq i+1) \tag{2}$$

In (2) $<p-2-i+j>_p$ represents modular arithmetic, so as others in the paper. An H-code on p = 7 is shown in Fig. 1.

## 2.2 H-Code Erasure Decoding

In [9], the author divided erasure decoding into two cases in term of erasure locations. Owing to spatial confined, the paper enumerates the most common one that column p is not erased but column 0 is erased. In this case, a decoder first searches for the starting point of the recovery chain which is determined by the erasure columns. Then the lost data elements in the same chain can be recovered by XOR operations within Eq. (2). Then all erasure symbols are fully recovered by computing other lost elements upon using the Zig-zag process. Figure 2 is the example of H-code encoding (p = 7). The starting point is $C_{0,0}$ and the decoder moves from ① to ⑪ following the direction of arrows.

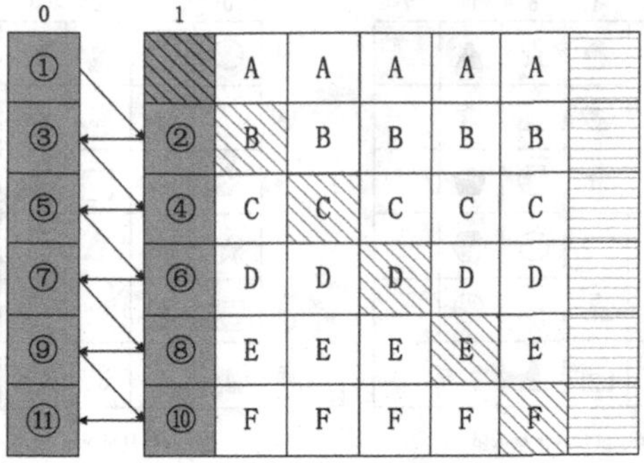

**Fig. 2.** Encoding of H-code (p = 7).

## 3    Eleven Code Encoding

An eleven code also consists of p + 1 columns which are extending from H-code, where the first and last columns are the same as H-code [10], i.e. all elements in column 0 are data and all elements of column p are parity. For Eleven code in this paper, which is verified by the parity check matrix, the parameter p we provided is prime and no less than five. Upon the construction of H-code, in which there has three kinds of elements–data, horizontal parity and anti-diagonal parity, the eleven code adds a new element, which is called diagonal parity. Although a new kind element is added, there has no extension on columns and rows because of its embedding among disks in a array as well. It is like X-code [12] based on shape when we just pay attention to the anti-diagonal parity and diagonal parity. However, the parity elements are not located in the last two rows but inserted to the array regularly. Due to the new parity elements occupying some data units, the encoding of H-code is no longer applies to a part of Eleven code. Algebraically, the encoding of Eleven code can be represented as:

Horizontal parity:

$$C_{i,p} = \sum_{j=0}^{p-1} C_{i,j} (j \neq i+1 \ and \ j \neq p-1-i) \tag{3}$$

Anti-diagonal parity:

$$C_{i,p-1-i} = \sum_{j=0}^{p-1} C_{<i+j>_p,j}$$
$$\left( j \neq p-1-i \ and \ j \neq \frac{p-1}{2} - \left[ \frac{i}{2} \right] + \frac{p-1}{2} \times mod(i,2) \right) \tag{4}$$

Diagonal parity:

$$C_{i,i+1} = \sum_{j=0}^{p-2} C_{j,<p-j+i>_p} \quad \left( j \neq \frac{p-1}{2} + \left[ \frac{i}{2} \right] - \frac{p-1}{2} \times mod(i,2) \right) \tag{5}$$

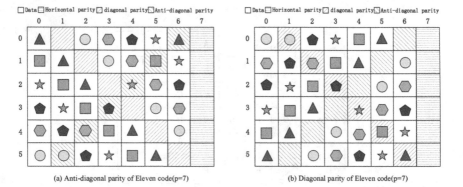

(a) Anti-diagonal parity of Eleven code(p=7)          (b) Diagonal parity of Eleven code(p=7)

**Fig. 3.**  Encoding of Eleven code (p = 7).

Construction of Eleven code for an 8-disk array that p = 7 is presented in Fig. 3. Because of the similarity on horizontal parity between H-code and Eleven code (Fig. 1(a)), the horizontal parity construction of Eleven code is not shown in this paper. Let $C_{i,j}$ represent the unit in row i, column j, as shown in Fig. 3. Horizontal parity in the last column is got by XOR operations. In contrast to H-code, there is $j \neq i+1$ $and\, j \neq$ $p-1-i$ in horizontal parity chains of Eleven code, such as row 0, $C_{0,7} = C_{0,0} \oplus C_{0,2} \oplus C_{0,3} \oplus C_{0,4} \oplus C_{0,5}$, where $j \neq 1$ and $j \neq 6$, namely, $C_{0,1}$ and $C_{0,6}$ are not involved in horizontal parity of row 0. Similarly, the other horizontal parity can be computed with (3). What calls for special attention is that $C_{0,1}$ no longer represents anti-diagonal parity but diagonal parity, and $C_{0,6}$ represents anti-diagonal parity. In general, the direction of parity chains is opposite to their parity elements location. For example, in (4), $C_{2,4} = C_{2,0} \oplus C_{3,1} \oplus C_{5,3} \oplus C_{0,5} \oplus C_{1,6}$, where $j \neq 4$ and $j \neq 2$, because $C_{4,2}$ storages anti-diagonal parity now, shown in Fig. 3(a). Intuitively, diagonal parity and anti-diagonal parity are symmetrical, but it is different. Take $C_{2,3}$ in Fig. 3(b) for example, $C_{0,2}$, $C_{1,1}$, $C_{2,0}$, $C_{3,6}$, $C_{5,4}$ are data elements participating in parity and $C_{4,5}$ expresses diagonal parity unit and not computed within XOR operations, which in virtue of (5), we calculate all other diagonal elements.

It is of utmost importance to verify the accuracy authentication of a code in order to justify the code to be used, and there are different methods to attest it. As presented in this section, we design a program to solve Eleven code's accuracy question. As stated above, Eleven code is of distance 4, which means it can recover any 3 erasures. Consequently, it is certain to correct any one or two errors. As for these two authentications, they can be comprehended obviously in Fig. 3.

We have clear evidence to recover one error from Fig. 3 so let us discuss two errors situations. We identify the double failure columns are $l_1$ and $l_2$ ($l_1 < l_2$). We can reconstruct the elements using the starting point: $C_{<l_1 - 1>_{(p-2)}, l_2}$. For example, when $l_1 = 3$ and $l_2 = 5$, the start points are $C_{2,\,5}$ we can recover the lost elements in the sequence of recovery: $C_{4,3} \rightarrow C_{1,5} \rightarrow C_{2,5} \rightarrow C_{0,3} \rightarrow C_{5,5} \rightarrow C_{0,5} \rightarrow C_{4,5} \rightarrow C_{2,3}$ $C_{3,3} \rightarrow C_{1,3} \rightarrow C_{3,5} \rightarrow C_{5,3}$. Other two errors situations are similar to this case.

Our verification focuses on 3-erasures. Similarly, we denote the three lost columns as $l_1$, $l_2$, $l_3$. In Fig. 3, it is obvious that the construction has symmetry. Thus, our priority is $l_1 = 0$ and $l_3 = p$, i.e., stripe 0 and stripe p are lost. It is obvious that there are all data elements or parity elements in them. We can recover them by the starting point: $C_{<2l_2-1>_p, 0}$ and $C_{<p-1-2l_2>_p, 0}$ with formula (3), (4), (5). While the above process just a case of erasure, other positions are difficult to use this method to solve so far. So will we adopt programing to calculate the accuracy.

**Acknowledgment.** This work was in part supported by Natural Science Foundation of China (NSFC) [NO. 61272450] and CERNET Innovation Project Grants [NGII20150410].

# References

1. Wu, C., He, X., Han, J., et al.: SDM: a stripe-based data migration scheme to improve the scalability of RAID-6. In: 2012 IEEE International Conference on Cluster Computing, pp. 284–292. IEEE (2012)

2. Fu, Y., Shu, J., Shen, Z., et al.: Reconsidering single disk failure recovery for erasure coded storage systems: optimizing load balancing in stack-level. IEEE Trans. Parallel Distrib. Syst. **27**(5), 1457–1469 (2016)
3. Pinheiro, E., Weber, W., Barroso, L.: Failure trends in a large disk drive population. In: Proceedings of the USENIX FAST 2007, San Jose, CA, February 2007
4. Schroeder, B., Gibson, G.: Disk failures in the real world: what does an MTTF of 1,000,000 hours mean to you? In: Proceedings of the USENIX FAST 2007, San Jose, CA, February 2007
5. Plank, J.S.: Erasure codes for storage applications. In: Tutorial Slides, Presented at the 4th USENIX Conference on File and Storage Technologies, FAST 2005, San Francisco, CA, USA, December 2005
6. Blaum, M., Roth, R.: On lowest density MDS codes. IEEE Trans. Inf. Theory **45**(1), 46–59 (1999)
7. Cassuto, Y., Bruck, J.: Cyclic lowest density MDS array codes. IEEE Trans. Inf. Theory **55** (4), 1721–1729 (2009)
8. Zhang, G., Li, K., Wang, J., et al.: Accelerate RDP RAID-6 scaling by reducing disk I/Os and XOR operations. IEEE Trans. Comput. **64**(1), 32–44 (2015)
9. Wu, C., et al.: H-code: a hybrid MDS array code to optimize partial stripe writes in RAID-6. In: Proceedings of the IPDPS 2011 (2011)
10. Corbett, P., English, B., Goel, A., Grcanac, T., Kleiman, S., Leong, J., Sankar, S.: Row-diagonal parity for double disk failure correction. In: Proceedings of the USENIX FAST 2004, San Francisco, CA, March 2004
11. Blaum, M., Brady, J., Bruck, J., Menon, J.: EVENODD: an efficient scheme for tolerating double disk failures in RAID architectures. IEEE Trans. Comput. **44**(2), 192–202 (1995)
12. Xu, L., Bruck, J.: X-code: MDS array codes with optimal encoding. IEEE Trans. Inf. Theory **45**(1), 272–276 (1999)
13. Hafner, J.L.: HoVer erasure codes for disk arrays. In: 2006 International Conference on Dependable Systems and Networks (DSN 2006), pp. 217–226, Philadelphia, Pennsylvania, USA, June 2006

# Parallel Peer Pressure Clustering Algorithm Based on Linear Algebra Computation

Jun Chen[1(✉)] and Peigang Zou[2]

[1] High Performance Computing Center,
Institute of Applied Physics and Computational Mathematics, Beijing, China
chenjun@iapcm.ac.cn
[2] Graduate School of China Academy of Engineering Physics, Beijing, China
Pg_zou@126.com

**Abstract.** Graph clustering is pervasive in emerging "big data" applications, and is known to be quite challenging to implement on distributed memory systems. In this work, we design and implement scalable distributed-memory algorithms for peer pressure clustering using the sparse matrix infrastructures of Combinatorial BLAS, where the peer pressure clustering algorithm is represent as sparse matrix computations. For settling ties, which is the most time-consuming step in this algorithm, we design a matrix-based algorithm and provide two parallel implementations. One is based on MPI model, and the other is a hybrid programming with MPI and OpenMP. Relying on matrix algebra building blocks, our algorithm exposes a high degree of parallelism and good scalability on distributed-memory platforms. For a real instance, when the input is a permuted R-MAT graph of scale 21 with self-loops added, our MPI implementation achieves up to 809.6x speedup on 1024 cores of a Dawning supercomputer, and the hybrid implementation with MPI and OpenMP obtains 949.5x speedup on 2048 cores of the same computer.

**Keywords:** Parallel computing · Large-scale graph · Peer pressure clustering · Linear algebra · Sparse matrix

## 1 Introduction

Graph clustering is the problem of determining natural groups with high connectivity in a graph. This can be useful in fields such as machine learning, data mining, pattern recognition, image analysis, and bioinformatics. There are numerous methods for graph clustering, many of which involve performing random walks through the graph. Here, we focus on a clustering algorithm called peer pressure clustering [1]. The increasing size of the large graph in various application encouraged development of many distributed-memory solvers as large-scale problems do not fit into a single node. The lack of distributed-memory graph clustering algorithms and implementations left a bottleneck in varied "big data" application. The current representative parallel implementation methods of peer pressure clustering contain SPARQL [2, 3] and STAR-P [4]. The SPARQL declarative query language is a powerful query language similar to

© Springer International Publishing AG 2017
Y. Dou et al. (Eds.): APPT 2017, LNCS 10561, pp. 105–116, 2017.
DOI: 10.1007/978-3-319-67952-5_10

SQL which operates on graphs specified in the RDF (short for Resource Description Framework) format, and includes innovative capabilities to match subgraph patterns within a semantic graph database, providing a powerful base upon which to implement complex graph algorithms for very large data. Star-P is a parallel implementation of the Matlab language with global array semantics, they demonstrated this with an implementation of peer pressure clustering using the sparse matrix infrastructure in STAR-P. Despite lots of active research, no published result achieves continuing speedups to thousands, or even hundreds of cores. This is an informal testimony to the hardness of parallelizing the peer pressure clustering problem in practice. Therefore, high performance scalable distributed-memory graph clustering algorithms, such as peer pressure clustering, are indeed needed in large distributed graphs.

This paper focuses on peer pressure clustering in a large graph. Peer pressure is a clustering algorithm based on the observation that for a given graph clustering the cluster assignment of a vertex will be the same as that of most of its neighbors. The algorithm starts with an initial cluster assignment, such as each vertex being in its own cluster. Each iteration performs an election at each vertex to select which cluster that vertex should belong to at the end of the iteration. The votes are the cluster assignments of its neighbors. Ties are settled by selecting the lowest cluster ID to maintain determinism here, but it also can be settled arbitrarily. The algorithm converges when two consecutive iterations have a tiny difference between them.

Matrix algebra has been recognized as a useful tool in graph theory [5] for nearly as long and references therein, However, matrices have not traditionally been used for practical computing with graphs, in part because a dense two dimensional matrix is not an efficient representation of a sparse graph. With the growth of efficient data structures and algorithms for sparse matrices, it has become possible to develop a practical matrix-based approach to computation on large, sparse graphs. The GraphBLAS standard (istc-bigdata.org/GraphBlas) is being developed to bring the potential of matrix based graph algorithms to the broadest possible audience. The GraphBLAS mathematically defines a core set of matrix-based graph operations that can be used to implement a wide class of graph algorithms in a wide range of programming environments.

In this paper, we have developed a matrix-based distributed-memory peer pressure clustering algorithm that employs sparse matrix-matrix multiplication (SpGEMM) to perform the election at each vertex to select which cluster that vertex should belong to in each iteration. So we focus on the SpGEMM algorithm called Sparse SUMMA [6–8], which uses two-dimensional block data distributions with serial hypersparse kernels(a matrix is hypersparse if the ratio of nonzeros to its dimension is asymptotically 0), is indeed highly flexible, scalable, and memory-efficient in the general case, and is the first to yield increasing speedup on an unbounded number of processors. It is because of the two-dimensional block distribution of sparse matrices where serial sections use a hypersparse kernel for scalability, the HyperSparseGEMM [9] that computing the product of two hypersparse matrices uses a new $O(nnz)$ data structure, called DCSC for doubly compressed sparse columns, which is explained in Sect. 4. After the election stage, what to do if two clusters tie for the maximum number of votes for a vertex? To settling ties, we designed a new parallel algorithm which was implemented both in MPI and in MPI-OpenMP to select the lowest cluster ID to maintain determinism. Lastly, we implemented this distributed-memory peer pressure clustering based on CombBLAS (short for Combinatorial BLAS [10]) which consists of a small but powerful set of linear algebra primitives specifically targeting graph and data mining applications. By representing the peer pressure clustering algorithm as sparse matrix computations, it allows structured representation of irregular data structures, decompositions, and irregular access patterns in graph applications. These modifications result in a highly-parallel peer pressure clustering algorithm that scales up to thousands of cores on Dawning supercomputer.

Our main contributions in this paper are as follows:

- We present a highly parallel algorithm for peer pressure clustering on distributed-memory system using matrix algebra.
- We present a matrix-based parallel algorithm for settling ties which is an important step in each iteration of the peer pressure clustering algorithm.
- We provide both a MPI implementation and a hybrid MPI-OpenMP implementation of the parallel peer pressure clustering. On synthetic graph, our algorithm was tested on a R-MAT [11] graph with 2.1 million vertices and 18.3 million edges.

The structure of the following sections will be as follows. Section 2 will introduce the standard peer pressure clustering algorithm and its matrix algebra representation. Section 3 will explain our parallel peer pressure clustering based on CombBLAS in detail. Section 4 will show the numerical experiments and discussions, and lastly the conclusion.

## 2 Preliminaries

In this paper, we represent a graph $G = (V, E)$ with $N$ vertices and $M$ edges by an $N \times N$ adjacency matrix which has the property $A(v_i, v_j) = 1$ if there is an edge $e_{ij}$ from vertex $v_i$ to vertex $v_j$ and is zero otherwise. The number of non-zero entries in $A$ corresponds to the number of edges in the graph $G$.

### 2.1   Standard Peer Pressure Clustering Algorithm

Peer pressure clustering [12] capitalizes on the fact that given any reasonable cluster approximation for the graph, a vertex's cluster assignment will be the same as the cluster assignment of the majority of its neighbors. If the incoming edges to each vertex in this graph are examined to determine from which cluster they originate, this clustering can be considered suboptimal. Each vertex has a majority of incoming edges originating from its own cluster. Traditionally, peer pressure clustering is performed by iteratively refining a cluster approximation for the graph. Given a cluster approximation, each vertex in the graph first votes for all of its neighbors to be in its current cluster. These votes are then tallied and a new cluster approximation is formed by moving vertices to the cluster for which they obtained the most votes. The algorithm typically terminates when a fixed point is reached (when two successive cluster approximations are identical). Algorithm 1 shows the recursive definition for peer pressure clustering.

**Algorithm** 1. Peer pressure clustering
**PeerPressure**$( G = (V, E), C_i )$
1  for $(u, v, w) \in E$
2    do $T(v)(C_i(u)) \leftarrow T(v)(C_i(u)) + w$
3  for $n \in V$
4    do $C_f(n) \leftarrow i : \forall j \in V : T(n)(j) \leq T(n)(i)$
5  if $C_i == C_f$ then return $C_f$
6  else return PeerPressure$( G = (V, E), C_i )$

In Algorithm 1, the loop at line 1 is responsible for the voting, and the loop at line 3 tallies those votes to form a new cluster approximation. It is assumed that the structure T is stored as an array of lists, which keeps track of, for each vertex, the number of votes that vertex gets for each cluster for which it receives votes.

In order to get things going with the peer pressure clustering algorithm, an initial cluster approximation must be chosen. For graphs that actually contain clusters, the solution arrived at by the algorithm is highly independent from the initial cluster approximation. For this reason, a naive starting approximation is that each vertex is in a cluster by itself. As shown below, where each vertex is in a cluster by itself, suffices to start things off: for v ∈ V, do Ci(v) = v.

In graphs where there is a large discrepancy between the out-degree of vertices, vertices with a large out-degree will have a larger influence on the cluster approximations. These vertices will have more votes in each cluster refinement because they have more outgoing edges. This can be easily remedied by normalizing the votes of each vertex to one. This can be done by summing up the weights of the outgoing edges of each vertex, and then dividing those weights by that sum.

Line 4 of Algorithm 1 does not specify what to do if two clusters tie for the maximum number of votes for a vertex. This can be done in a deterministic manner by selecting the cluster with the lowest number. This deterministic method also helps to speed the algorithm to convergence by having all vertices choose the same "leader" for their cluster early in the algorithm.

## 2.2    Peer Pressure Clustering Using Matrix Algebra

While the graph is represented as a weighted adjacency matrix, $G = A: \mathbb{R}_+^{N \times N}$, the clustering algorithm can be performed in the same manner. Let $C : \mathbb{B}^{N \times N}$ be the cluster approximation, where if $c_{ij} == 1$, then vertex $j$ is in cluster $i$. With this representation, voting can be expressed as a simple matrix multiplication: T = CA. Here T represents a tallying matrix where if $t_{ij} == k$, then there are $k$ votes for vertex $j$ to be in cluster $i$. Once the votes have been performed, the new clusters need to be selected. This can be done with the following operations: m = T max. (m is an array where each array element stores the count of maximum vote in each column), $C_f$ = m. == T (Performing logical AND operation between array m and each row of matrix T to get the cluster approximation matrix $C_f$ in this iteration). Here the max vote for each vertex in each cluster is found, then the cluster approximation is set appropriately according to that value. Algorithm 2 shows the matrix-based peer pressure clustering algorithm. Line 2 performs the voting, and lines 3 and 4 tally those votes to form a new cluster approximation.

**Algorithm 2.** Peer pressure clustering matrix formulation

**PeerPressure_M(** $G = A : R_+^{N \times N}, C_i : B^{N \times N}$ **)**

1   $T : R_+^{N \times N} \quad C_f : B^{N \times N} \quad m : R_+^{N}$

2   $T = C_i A$

3   $m = T \max.$

4   $C_f = m. = T$

5   if $C_i = C_f$ then return $C_f$

6   else return PeerPressure_M(G, $C_f$)

As before, an initial approximation must be selected. If each vertex is in a cluster by itself, with the cluster number being equal to the vertex number, then $C_i = I$. Normalizing the out-degrees of the vertices in the graph corresponds to normalizing the rows of the adjacency matrix. This can be done as below: w = A + ., A = 1/w . × A. Settling ties for votes in this clustering algorithm requires selecting the lowest numbered cluster with the highest number of votes. In many linear algebra packages, this simply corresponds to a call to max, finding the location of the maximum values in each column. Typically, the location corresponds to the first maximum value in that column, or the smallest cluster number among those who tie for maximums.

### 2.3   Previous Works on Parallel Peer Pressure Clustering

We are aware of only two results on distributed-memory peer pressure clustering. Kevin Deweese et al. [3] presented a method to find a global graph metric, clustering using the peer pressure algorithm, using SPARQL, and they had targeted their code for a dataset from the Mayo Clinic "Smackdown" project to help identify potential disease cause. John R. Gilbert et al. [4] argued that many of the tools of high-performance numerical computing – in particular, parallel algorithms and data structures for computation with sparse matrices – can form the nucleus of a robust infrastructure for parallel computing on graphs, they demonstrated this with an implementation of peer pressure clustering using the sparse matrix infrastructure in STAR-P. All the parallel implementations listed above were scaled up to 128 cores at most (SPARQL: scale up to 64, STAR-P: scale up to 128), and showed no specific speedup and scalability. However, it implied that they did not actually achieve good parallel performance using STAR-P [4].

# 3 Parallel Peer Pressure Clustering

## 3.1 Data Distribution and Storage

We use CombBLAS framework which distributes its sparse matrices on a two dimensional $p_r \times p_c$ processor grid. Processor $P(i,j)$ stores the sub-matrix $A_{ij}$ of dimensions $(m / p_r) \times (n / p_c)$ in its local memory. The Combinatorial BLAS uses the doubly compressed sparse columns (DCSC) format to store its local submatrices for scalability. DCSC is a further compressed version of CSC where repetitions in the column pointers array, which arise from empty columns, are not allowed. Only columns that have at least one nonzero are represented, together with their column indices. The HyperSparseGEMM operates on the strictly $O(nnz)$ doubly compressed sparse column (DCSC) data structure, and its time complexity does not depend on the matrix dimension, as opposed to $O(n\sqrt{p} + nnz)$ memory across all processors for CSC format. Above all, DCSC is essentially a sparse array of sparse columns, whereas CSC is a dense array of sparse columns.

## 3.2 Parallel Peer Pressure Clustering Algorithm

We present a parallel algorithm for peer pressure clustering on distributed-memory system using CombBLAS primitives, showed in Algorithm 3, and design a parallel algorithm to settling ties which is an important step in the peer pressure clustering.

**Algorithm 3** Parallel peer pressure clustering
**Input**: *Graph* $A : R_+^{N \times N}$, *and an initial approximation* $C_i : B^{N \times N}$.
**Output**: *A matrix-based clustering result.*
    **Procedure** Peerssure(G= $A : R_+^{N \times N}, C_i : B^{N \times N}$)

1. SpParMat A, $C_i$ ;
2. DenseParVe rowsums=A.Reduce(Row,plus<double>); //*reduce to Row,columns are collapsed to single entries*
3. rowsums.Apply(multinv<double>);
4. A.DimScale(Row, rowsums); //*normalize A, scale each column with given vector*
5. while $C_i$ != T do

6.    SpParMat T=SpGEMM( $C_i$ ,A); //*vote*
7.    Renormalize(SpParMat &T); //*renormalize T*
8.    settling_ties(SpParMat &T); //*settling ties*

Line 1–4 perform the process of assuring vertices have equal votes using 3 primitives in Combinatorial BLAS including Reduce(), Apply(), and Dimscale(), Line 5-8 represent the iterations of clustering, particularly, line 6 is responsible for the step of voting, Line 7 shows the step of renormalize, which assures the elements in T matrix remain to 1 or 0. Line 8 perform the step of settling ties that select the lowest numbered cluster with the highest number of votes in T matrix which shows the voting result in this iteration. The following sections will describe the parallel algorithms used in these steps.

### 3.3   Algorithm Expansion

#### (1)  Parallel voting

For voting, we employ the SpGEMM algorithm called Sparse SUMMA which is showed in Algorithm 4. The coarseness of the algorithm can be adjusted by changing the block size $1 \leq b \leq \gcd(k/p_r, k/p_c)$. The pseudo code, however, requires $b$ to evenly divide $k/p_r$ and $k/p_c$ for ease of presentation.

**Algorithm 4** SpGEMM algorithm

**Input:** $A \in S^{m \times k}, B \in S^{k \times n}$ :sparse matrices distributed on a $p_r \times p_c$ processor grid.

**Output:** $C \in S^{m \times n}$ : the product $AB$ ,similarly distributed.
Procedure SparseSUMMA(A,B,C)
1   for all processors $P(i, j)$ in parallel do
2     $B_{ij} \leftarrow (B_{ij})^T$
3   for all q=1 to $k/b$ do //blocking parameter b evenly divides $k/p_r$ and $k/p_c$
4       $c = (q \cdot b)/(k/p_c)$ //the broadcasting processor column
5       $r = (q \cdot b)/(k/p_r)$ //the broadcasting processor row
6       $lcols = (q \cdot b) \bmod c : ((q+1) \cdot b) \bmod c$ //local column
7       $lrows = (q \cdot b) \bmod r : ((q+1) \cdot b) \bmod r$ //local row
8       $A^{rem} \leftarrow Broadcast(A_{ic}(:, lcols), P(i,:))$
9       $B^{rem} \leftarrow Broadcast(B_{rj}(:, lrows), P(:, j))$
10      $C_{ij} \leftarrow C_{ij} + HyperSparseGEMM(A^{rem}, B^{rem})$
11     $B_{ij} \leftarrow (B_{ij})^T$     // Restore the original B.

The *Broadcast* $(A_{ic}, P(i, :))$ syntax means that the owner of $A_{ic}$ becomes the root and broadcasts its submatrix to all the processors on the *ith* processor row. Similarly for *Broadcast* $(B_{rj}, P(:, j))$, the owner of $B_{rj}$ broadcasts its sub matrix to all the processors on the *jth* processor column. In lines 6–7, the local column (for **A**) and row (for **B**) ranges for matrices that are to be broadcast during that iteration. They are significant only for the broadcasting processors, which can be determined implicitly from the first parameter of Broadcast. Here **B** is indexed by columns as opposed to rows, because it has already been locally transposed in line 2. This makes indexing faster since local submatrices are stored in the column-based DCSC sparse data structure. The HyperSparseGEMM in line 10 uses an outer-product formulation whose time complexity is $O(nzc(A) + nzr(B) + flops(AB) \times lg(ni))$, where $nzc(A)$ is the number of columns of **A** that are not entirely zero, $nzr(B)$ is the number of rows of **B** that are not entirely zero, $flops(AB)$ is the number of nonzero arithmetic operations required to compute the product $AB$, and $ni$ is the number of indices $i$ for which $A(:, i) \neq \emptyset$ and $B(i, :) \neq \emptyset$. The extra $lg(ni)$ factor in the time complexity expression originates from the priority queue that is used to merge $ni$ outer products on the fly. The overall memory requirement of this algorithm is the asymptotically optimal $O(nnz(A) + nnz(B) + nnz(C))$, independent of either matrix dimensions or flops.

## (2)  **Renormalization**

In this step, we leverage two primitives in CombBLAS to assure the elements in **T** matrix remain to 1 or 0. As shown in Algorithm 5.

> **Algorithm** 5 Renormalize the T matrix
> Renormalize (SpParMat &T)
>     DenseParVec colmax=T.reduce(Column,max.);
>     T.DimApply(column,colmaxs,equal_to<double>);

## (3)  **Parallel settling**

We design and implement matrix-based algorithms to settle ties in a MPI version and a hybrid MPI-OpenMP version respectively, showed in Algorithms 6 and 7. In this stage, we select the lowest numbered cluster with the highest number of votes.

**Algorithm** 6. Settling ties with MPI
Settling_ties_MPI(SpParMat &T)
1   for all processors $P(i, j)$ in parallel do
2       vector<int> v=T.CreateVec(); //*create a vector tallying the processor number.*
3       MPI_Allreduce(v,min_v,k,MPI_INT,MPI_INT,..);
            // *do MPI_Allreduce on every processor column.*
4       T.PruneMat(min_v);  // *generate clustering results.*

**Algorithm** 7. Settling ties with MPI-OpenMP
Settling_ties_MPIOpenMP(SpParMat &T)
1   for all processors $P(i, j)$ in parallel do
2       DO *pp*=1, *num_threads* parallel with OpenMP
            // *num_threads is the number of threads per process.*
3           vector<int> v=T.CreatVec();
                //*create a vector tallying the processor number.*
4       ENDDO for pp
5       MPI_Allreduce(v,min_v,k,MPI_INT,MPI_INT,..);
            // *do MPI_Allreduce on every processor column.*
6       Do *pp*=1, *num_threads* parallel with OpenMP
7           T.PruneMat(min_v);  // *generate clustering results.*
8       END DO for *pp*

In Algorithm 6, CreatVec() constructs a vector where each element is corresponding to each column in **T** matrix. If the values in some columns contain 1, then its processor ID will be tallied to its corresponding element in the vector. Otherwise, the maximal integer will be tallied. In line 3, MPI_Allreduce() is executed on every processor column to select the lowest numbered processor with the corresponding value of 1 in each vector of every processor column. In line 4 (PruneMat()), a new matrix is generated which represents the clustering result in this iteration according to the new vector, called min_v, generated in line 3.

Algorithm 7 is the hybrid MPI-OpenMP implementation of our ties-settling algo-rithm. We provide the intra-node multithreading in step 1 (CreatVec()) and step 2 (PruneMat()) using OpenMP respectively.

# 4   Numerical Experiments

## 4.1   Environment and the Input Graph

A Dawning supercomputer is used for our experiments. Its nodes are interconnected with Intel Omni-Path network. Each compute node is equipped with 64 GB RAM and two 12-core 2.5 GHz Intel E5-2680 processors. Its MPI implementation is based on Mvapich2. We used OpenMP for intra-node multithreading and compiled the code with icc −O2 −fopenmp flags. In our experiments, we only used square process grids because rectangular grids are not supported in CombBLAS now. For the settling ties part with MPI-OpenMP implementation, we used 8 threads per MPI process and each MPI process was placed on a processor. All MPI processes perform local computation followed by synchronized communication rounds.

The input is a permuted R-MAT graph of scale 21, with self-loops added, con-taining 2.1 million vertices and 18.3 million edges.

## 4.2   Experiment Results

### (1)   MPI implementation

Figure 1 shows the total run time of MPI implementation. It took less than a minute to cluster the graph on 1024 cores, while more than 12 h was spent to cluster on a single processor. Our algorithm achieves up to 809.6x speedup on 1024 cores. Figure 2 shows the speedup gained from 4 to 1024 cores for this version. It is a linear scale.

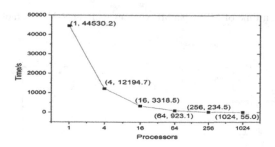

**Fig. 1.** The run time of MPI version when clustering an R-MAT graph of scale 21.

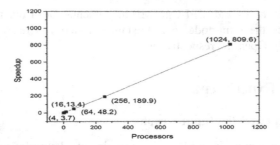

**Fig. 2.** The speedup of MPI version when clustering an R-MAT graph of scale 21.

## (2) MPI-OpenMP implementation

Figures 3 and 4 respectively show the total runtime and speedup of our MPI-OpenMP implementation. On 2048 cores, we were able to cluster this graph in less than a minute. The same graph takes more than 12 h to cluster on a single processor. Our hybrid implementation achieves up to 949.5x speedup on 2048 cores of a Dawning supercomputer.

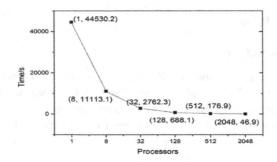

**Fig. 3.** The run time of MPI-OpenMP version with an R-MAT graph of scale 21.

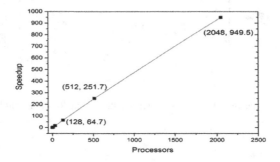

**Fig. 4.** The speedup of MPI-OpenMP version with an R-MAT graph of scale 21.

## 4.3  Discussions

From the above speedup figures of the MPI version and hybrid version, it shows the good scalability of the two implementations. The parallel efficiency of the MPI version running on 1024 cores of the Dawning supercomputer achieved 79.1%, compared with 46.4% on 2048 cores for hybrid version. For the hybrid version with MPI and OpenMP, the parallel efficiency on the cores from 8 to 2048 is small declining from 50% to 46.4%.

In our current MPI version, there is a limit on the core numbers can be used. It should be the product of two numbers of the same value. There are two reason causes this limit. One reason is that the number of columns is equal to the number of rows. The other is that the current version based on CombBLAS uses even distribution between processor cores. For the same reasons, the number of cores that the hybrid version can be used is also limited. To provide more flexibility on the number of cores can be used is the future work.

## 5  Conclusion

Results of the experiments obtain satisfied speedup and parallel efficiency, and prove the feasibility and validity of this distributed algorithm for peer pressure clustering. In this work, we showed that matrix-algebraic primitives enabled our algorithms to achieve high speedups to thousands of processors.

Currently, our settling ties step together make up more than 99% of the total running time. Future work includes developing a faster, lower communication algorithm for settling ties, that dominate the performance at large concurrencies in both MPI and MPI-OpenMP implementation.

## References

1. Shah, V.B.: An interactive system for combinatorial scientific computing with an emphasis on programmer productivity, Dissertation. University of California, Santa Barbara (2007)
2. Techentin, R.W., et al.: Implementing iterative algorithms with SPARQL. Edbt/icdt workshops 2014, pp. 216–223 (2014)
3. Deweese, K., et al.: Graph clustering in SPARQL. In: SIAM Workshop on Network Science, vol. 34, pp. 930–941 (2013)
4. Gilbert, J.R., Reinhardt, S., Shah, V.B.: High-performance graph algorithms from parallel sparse matrices. In: Kågström, B., Elmroth, E., Dongarra, J., Waśniewski, J. (eds.) PARA 2006. LNCS, vol. 4699, pp. 260–269. Springer, Heidelberg (2007). doi:10.1007/978-3-540-75755-9_32
5. Harary, F.: Graph Theory. Addison-Wesley, Boston (1969)
6. Buluç, A., Gilbert, J.R.: Highly parallel sparse matrix-matrix multiplication. Computer Science, abs/1006.2183 (2010)
7. Buluç, A., Gilbert, J.R.: Parallel sparse matrix-matrix multiplication and indexing: Implementation and experiments. SIAM J. Sci. Comput. **34**(4), C170–C191 (2012)

8. Buluç, A., Gilbert, J.R.: Challenges and advances in parallel sparse matrix-matrix multiplication. In: 37th International Conference on Parallel Processing, ICPP 2008, pp. 503–510. IEEE (2008)
9. Buluç, A., Gilbert, J.R.: On the representation and multiplication of hypersparse matrices. In: IEEE International Symposium on Parallel and Distributed Processing, IPDPS 2008, pp. 1–11. IEEE (2008)
10. Buluç, A., Gilbert, J.R.: The combinatorial BLAS: design, implementation, and applications. Int. J. High Perform. Comput. Appl. **25**(4), 496–509 (2011)
11. Chakrabarti, D., Zhan, Y., Faloutsos, C.: R-MAT: a recursive model for graph mining. In: SDM, vol. 4, pp. 442–446 (2004)
12. Jeremy, K., Gilbert, J. (eds.): Graph Algorithms in the Language of Linear Algebra, vol. 22. SIAM, Philadelphia (2011)

# A Concurrent Skip List Balanced on Search

Fei Mei[1], Qiang Cao[1(✉)], Fei Wu[1], and Hongyan Li[2]

[1] Wuhan National Laboratory for Optoelectronics,
Key Laboratory of Information Storage System, Ministry of Education,
Huazhong University of Science and Technology, Wuhan, China
{meifei,caoqiang,wufei}@hust.edu.cn
[2] HuBei University of Economics, Wuhan, China

**Abstract.** We introduce a skip list, T-list, that updates the index on the search process by recording critical positions in the traverse of the index nodes. T-list uses a step counter to decide when and where to build a new index node and guarantees that the index node is generated in critical position unlike the probabilistic skip list, resulting in an efficient index structure. Meanwhile T-list does not enforce strong constraints to the overall structure unlike the deterministic skip list, thus eliminates a lot of maintaining work. Worst case in T-list can be efficiently repaired by a few requests that traverse the most part of list. Building a new index node in T-list only modifies the contents of two adjacent nodes, enabling the algorithm friendly to concurrent accessing. Experimental results show that compared to the skip list used in a popular application - LevelDB, T-list can construct a more efficient and stable index structure and the insertion and search performances are improved by 17.8% and 33.3% respectively. T-list also scales well with the threads number in the multi-core machine.

**Keywords:** Skip list · Concurrent list · Key value store · Index structure

## 1 Introduction

Skip list is a structure that is easy to implement and allows fast search and insertion, originally introduced by Pugh et al. [15] as an alternative to the balanced tree. A standard skip list comprises multiple layers of nodes. The bottom layer contains the inserted nodes each with a unique key and the user data (i.e., value). The nodes in a higher layer can be regarded as a subset of the lower layer but only contains the keys and pointers to other nodes and act as indexes. A new node is first inserted into the bottom layer and gets a height in probability, then in each layer within the height a indexing node with the same key is also created. Due to the simplicity of concept and easiness of implementation, skip list has been adopted by many LSM-tree based key-value stores such as BigTable [1], HBase [7], Cassandra [11], LevelDB [4], and MemSQL [17]. In different use scenarios it plays different roles. For example, in LevelDB the new

Y. Dou et al. (Eds.): APPT 2017, LNCS 10561, pp. 117–128, 2017.
DOI: 10.1007/978-3-319-67952-5_11

inserted key-value pairs are stored in a skip list that is a part of the whole user data, while MemSQL uses skip list as a secondary index [12] for its clustered user data.

State-of-the-art implementations of skip lists are categorized into two classes with respective shortcomings. The first one is styled by the implementations based on the original idea that generates height by probability, called probabilistic skip list. Although probability mechanism can expect to obtain the $logN$ search complexity [15], it lacks stability and is not easy for purposely optimizing, such as space locality, because a new node gets its height independently without considering the status of the nearby nodes and is not to be changed in the future once determined. Defective index nodes that degrade the indexing efficiency can also be generated unpredictably. The other class consists of the implementations that enforce a set of predefined rules and constraints to the structure, called deterministic skip list. On each update to a node, the deterministic list forcedly adjusts its whole structure to restore the defined rules. Since the adjusting process leads to many check operations and must maintains information of nearby nodes, the deterministic list is complex to implement and not friendly to concurrent accesses in multi-thread environments.

In this paper we present T-list, a skip list construction algorithm that maintains loose rules on the overall index structure when new node joins, but strengthen it gradually on the processing of search requests. Since an insertion operation always executes a search phase to determine the position for inserting, the index structure can also be built up under 100% insertion workload. When processing operations that may change the structure, T-list only modifies at most two nodes on a layer, making it multi-thread friendly because a write operation only involves locking of two adjacent nodes on a single layer. T-list may generate thin index structure for particular requests sequence. For instance, T-list does generate index for a reversely ordered sequence of keys because the search phase for each insertion needs only on step. However, the index can be built up if some search requests that need more steps are processed. In other words, T-list generates the index on need, which can be a better choice for the memory component of the LSM-tree based key-value stores mentioned above.

The rest of the paper is organized as follows. In Sect. 2 we briefly discuss the related works. The design and implementation are detailed in Sect. 3. Section 4 presents the evaluation results. At last we conclude the work and discuss future plans in Sect. 5.

## 2    Background and Related Works

Three basic operations are defined on a general list structure, insertion, search and deletion. The insertion and deletion operations always need a search phase to determine where to insert the new node or which node to delete. Based on the basic operations, skip list has been researched for fast searches as well as for favorable concurrent insertions.

Pugh et al. first presented the skip list [15] as an alternative to tree structure for its expected $logN$ search complexity and implemented a lock-based concurrent version [14]. Munro et al. [13] proposed to enforce pre-defined rules on the skip list, to achieve deterministic structure. One of deterministic structure is the 1–2 skip list that adjusts the structure each time after inserting a new node to hold the rules non-violated by recursively inspecting the nearby information until the whole structure became balanced. Another construction method introduced in this paper was the top-down 1-2-3 skip list, which can be regarded as a remedy policy that repairs the structure in the next time and the distance of any two nodes is allowed to be 3 even if it has the equivalent property with 1-2 skip list. T-list is similar to the top-down list in that it moves the index building work to the search phase, and the insertion operation finishes immediately after linking the new node into the bottom layer. However, the top-down list must check the total number of nodes in the gap from which the search process descends, and adjusts the structure to keep the nodes between the gap not exceeding the predefined value (i.e., 3 for the 1-2-3 list). Instead, T-list counts the steps when the search progresses and raises the height of a node when the steps reaches to the predefined value without inspecting all nodes between the gap. Other works are optimizations based on the above concepts and most of them focus on concurrent environment. Herlihy designed the lock-based skip list [10] that is built on the lazy-list [8], which acquires locks for all nodes that need to be modified when inserting or removing nodes. Non-blocking concurrent mechanisms [3,5,9,19] achieves concurrency by using atomic instructions. Skip lists are also used in network environments. Singh et al. presented the algorithms for achieving concurrency in a distributed deterministic 1-2 skip list [18] and a self-stabilizing peer-to-peer network maintenance algorithm is designed by Clouser et al. [2].

Except the above works, skip lists are also adopted by key-value stores as the in-memory component. For example, LevelDB, a popular key-value store, implements a probabilistic skip list (Lev-list) as the in-memory structure [4]. In Lev-list a configurable variable referred to as *branch* (default to 4) controls the general structure. A new node gets a height by the probability related to the value of branch. Such as, the branch value set to 4 means the height will be 2 in probability of $\frac{1}{4}$, and be 3 in probability of $\frac{1}{4^2}$, and so on. This results a list in which a layer expects to have 1/4 nodes of the layer under it, and the list height expects to be $log_4N$ in which N is the total number of nodes in the bottom layer. Lev-list does not explicitly implement deletion operation but instead marks the node as deleted, known as logical deletion [3,6,16]. The deletion marker is also useful in LevelDB for removing keys that exist on the disk. The lifetime of Lev-list is temporary, as it is periodically transformed and destroyed, and a new empty list is created to receive new requests.

With a study of these researches and the practical implementations, we found that the probabilistic skip list is easy to implement because of no need to maintain rules on the overall structure, but has degraded performance for its non-perfect index structure, while deterministic skip list is the other way around.

The design of T-list aims to resolve the shortcomings that exist in the probabilistic skip list and the deterministic skip list, in order to make a better trade off in practical use case such as LSM-tree environment. Probabilistic skip list builds the index without knowledge of the nearby nodes, leading to defective indexing nodes that degrade the search efficiency. In the contrary, deterministic skip list enforces special rules and constraints on the structure and performs check operations based on the intensity of nearby nodes, leading to heavy maintaining work. T-list decouples the insertion operation to two distinct phases, search and linking. The search phase traverses the list to find a bottom node after which the new node should be linked. In the process of traversing, indexes are built by the traverse steps. The linking phase simply links the new node to the bottom layer.

## 3  Design and Implementation

### 3.1  Structure Overview

We start with a figurative description of the structure overview of T-list. First let us assume a sorted link list without indexing structure on it. For each search request, it must traverse the list nodes one by one until it finds a key equal or greater than the requested key. Now we regard each node as a station, and the link between two adjacent nodes as a path. The search request is performed by a traveler who walks along the path station by station to find the target station that contains the requested key. Walking from one station to the next is counted as one step. Each time when he have walked a fixed number of steps (e.g. two) he will want to build a higher station in the higher path that is more convenient. Next time when the traveler accepts a search request he will first walk along the higher path on which he walks faster than along the lower one, until to a station he must go down. The point is that when he traverses on the higher path he as well keeps building more higher stations if he walks the fixed number of steps. Insertion request is served in such a way that after finding the insertion position on the bottom path the new node (station) is simply linked.

In the remained of the paper, when we say a node or station on the bottom path, they have the same meaning, except that node is used when we refer to a key while stations is used when we refer to traversing. Figure 1 shows a simple T-list example with 8 nodes/stations on the bottom path. Each station on other paths at the same vertical line contains a pointer to the node so the key can be accessed quickly anywhere on the search process.

The fixed number of steps in the above description is defined as *span* of the list, which has the equal role as the *branch* in LevelDB. A *span* of two means that a higher station is to be built every time when the traveler walks two steps. All stations on the same vertical line are transportable. That is, each station contains two pointers to its upper and lower stations respectively. The header stations plays the same role as the others except that it does not contain a key. The last station in each path points to null. The height of the list is determined

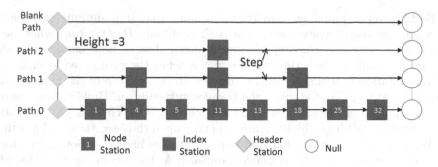

**Fig. 1.** A T-list example with the span configured to 2. A step on a path usually means two steps on its lower path.

by the highest path. A blank path above the highest path is set with the header station as the last station. The blank path is used for assisting adding station and is not counted for the height.

## 3.2   Search Procedure

Before introducing other operations, we first give a brief description of how to search a key in T-list. Search operation in T-list has two versions. One is called *PureTravel* that works the same way as in common skip lists. The other is called *BuildTravel* that is the core function in T-list, which plays the role of constructing the indexing structure.

PureTravel begins from the highest path and descends at a station if it is the last station on the path or its next station contains a greater key than the target, until finally it descends to the bottom path. Traveling on the bottom path will report the search result. If no key is found, the last node that has a lesser key than the target will be returned (Fig. 2 targeting the key 26), otherwise the node with the key matching the target is returned. Matching can also be met on other paths above the bottom, in which case the matching node is returned immediately.

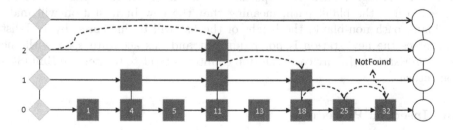

**Fig. 2.** *PureTravel to Find the Key 26.* The traveler begins at path 2 and ends at path 0 with the node 25, because the next node of node 25 has a greater key than the target.

BuildTravel is based on PureTravel, besides that it maintains two markers when the search traverses on the path and calls *BuildStation* when necessary. One marker is the step counter which indicates how many steps the traveler has walked. Each time the counter reaches the configured *span* value, the BuildStation function is called to build a station on top of the current station (referred to as *base_station*) the traveler suspends on. BuildStaion assures whether the station should be indeed built (check). If the check is passed, a station is built, i.e. adding a higher station on the top of the *base_station*. The other marker is a station pointer that always points to the higher station from which the traveler lastly descends (*pre_higher_station*). At the beginning of the search, the *pre_higher_station* points to the header station on the blank path. The step is reset to 0 each time the descending occurs or after the BuildStation is called. An example is illustrated in Fig. 3, in which we assume the key 33 is searched and the *pre_higher_station* is pointing to the node 18 in path 1 when the traveler walks to 32. At this time, BuildStation is called since the step counter reaches 2.

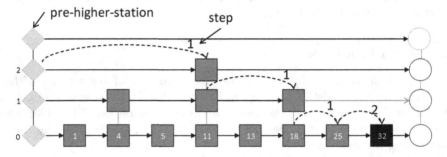

**Fig. 3.** When searching to the node 32, the step counter reaches 2 (span of the list), so the BuildStation function is called to build station on it and the new station will be linked after pre_higher_station (node 18 in the path 1)

The BuildStation function only needs the *base_station* and *pre_higher_station* to know where to build the new station. It first checks whether the station should be really built. If the station next to the *base_station* has a higher station, the checking would fail and the building operation is canceled, avoiding redundant station in the higher path. In a special case when the check is passed and the higher path is the blank path, meaning that the new built station will make the blank path non-blank, the height of the list will be increased by 1. T-list guarantees the new station is not redundant and has accurate *span* with the *pre_higher_station*. In any case, the step counter is reset to 0 after the BuildStation returns.

### 3.3    Insertion Procedure

The list is initiated as an empty list that only has the header node pointing to null. This empty list still has a path 0 (the bottom path) and a blank path above it, and its height is regarded as 1. In other words, the path 0 of an empty list has the same structure as the blank path.

An insertion operation is decoupled to two phases: (1) Searching the position on the path 0 where the new key should be placed, and (2) Linking the new node into the location. The location should be between two adjacent nodes that the previous one has the key lesser than the new key and the next one has the key greater than the new key, or the next one is null. The search phase is the main work of the insertion operation and is accomplished by BuildTravel in our implementation, and the linking phase is a simple operation just linking the new node in the found location.

The BuildTravel is called in the search phase of insert operation because potentially higher stations may need to be built as the new joined node increases the number of the bottom stations. Theoretically, the stations built by Build-Travel have no benefits to the calling search process. However, the new node can be taken into consideration in the later building procedures if any request executes BuildTravel across it. There can be a T-list with a thin index structure even if the path 0 has many nodes under special workloads, but this situation is the result that the processed requests need no long travelling. The thin index structure can grow to be strong if a few requests have traveled most part of the list. For example, T-list provides a Perfect function that at most needs $logN$ requests to make a perfect index structure on a bare list that only has one path (path 0) with N nodes. One can execute the insertion process by calling Pure-Travel, and running the BuildTravel with background threads to build index. However, our experiments showed that running the BuildTravel background is not always prompt to satisfy search efficiency of the insertion.

## 3.4    Concurrent Operations

We implement a lock-based concurrent mechanism for multiple threads to operate the list without breaking the list structure. As the PureTravel only reads the memory content, we leave the threads free to do such operations. The concurrent mechanism focuses on resolving multiple threads contenting for adding stations to the list.

In summary, the BuildStation operation and the linking operation are two actions that modify the structure of T-list. The BuildStation only adds new stations in non-bottom paths at a time, while the linking only adds a new station (node) to the bottom path. With this property in mind, we design a simple control mechanism that allocates one lock for each path, defined as path lock(PL). Actually, fine grained lock can be applied on T-list to enable multiple threads operating concurrently on a same path. There are totally the max_height (i.e. 40) number of PLs initiated for use, each responsible for a path.

The following steps are executed by a thread in order to add a station.

(i) Decide to add a station. This indicates that the thread has determined to add a station X on path $i$ between two adjacent stations A and B.

(ii) Acquire the lock on path $i$ (PL[$i$]). If other threads are changing the structure on path $i$, this thread must wait.

(iii) Reconfirm the real location of the new station if the lock is got. There is possibility that other threads have added stations between A and B, so it is necessary to reconfirm whether it is needed to add this new station and where to add it. The reconfirming is done by looking forward the path $i$ from station A until it meets a station whose key is greater than that of station X. This station is marked as station B', and the station previous to it is marked as station A'.
(iv) Check if it is really needed to add station between station A' and B'. If the check is passed, the station would be linked between A' and B', otherwise nothing is done.
(v) Release PL[$i$].

When a thread decides to call BuildStation on a particular path $i(0 \leq i \leq height)$, it first records the station (station A) after which the new one will be linked, and then acquires the lock PL[$i$]. After path $i$ has been locked, no other threads can change the structure on it, therefor the following operations can be done safely with no disturbances. However, other threads may have added new stations on path $i$ when the PL is acquired, and the real position may turn to be the new station added by other threads. In this case if the thread directly adds its new station, the structure would be broken. To avoid this, a look-forward operation is done to find the real position. After the look-forward, the new station can be safely added, because this operation is done under the lock, other threads can not disturb the operation.

### 3.5 Other Implementation Issues

In this section we talk about some other implementation issues in T-list. Deletion operation in the prototype of T-list is implemented by logically marking the node as deleted, while all the stations on it are preserved for indexing. There are physical deletion discusses in the top-down skip list [13] and other works [3,10]. In the practical use case as in LevelDB, the deletion operation is a special insertion operation targeting the same key but replaces the value with a deletion marker, which can be regarded as a logical deletion mechanism. We also implement Perfect function to build a perfect indexing structure for the list. This function traverses all the paths from bottom to top by a modified BuildTravel function. The Destroy function is a cleanup procedure after the list life ends. It releases all the resources the list has acquired from the OS.

## 4 Evaluation

We evaluate T-list with the following purposes:

- Examine the performance of T-list for different workloads.
- Verify the structure property generated by T-list.
- Evaluate the performance scalability for increasing number of the threads.

In the basic evaluation experiments, we compare the results with the skip-list used in LevelDB, which is a single-thread version. To make the comparison fair, we extract the code only related to the skip list structure from LevelDB and make it only serve integral keys. This list will be referred to as Lev-list in the following text. The configuration of *branch* in Lev-list had the same effect as the *span* in T-list, and their values had the equivalent influence on the structure, so we used the word *span* to refer both configurations. We then evaluate the scalability for increasing threads of T-list.

Our evaluation experiments are executed on a machine equipped with Intel Xeon Processor E3-1270 v2 (8M Cache, 3.50 GHz) which supports eight threads and four 8-GB DDR3 memory cards. Each experiment is run 5 times and the average value is computed as the final result.

### 4.1 Performance

We used three kinds of workloads to evaluate the performances of the two structures.

(1) 100% put. All operations are insertion requests.
(2) 100% get. All operations are search requests.
(3) 2:8 hybrid. For each incoming request, the probability of insertion is 20% and search is 80%.

The put workload fills the list from blank to the given size by random keys with uniform distribution. The get workload searches a million random keys from the list that is filled by the put workload. The hybrid workload fills the list in the same manner as the put workload, except that a lot of search requests are mixed in the process. The size of the list is varied in different number of keys(from $10^3$ to $10^8$). The *span* is configured with two different values, 2 and 4. Each experiment selects a workload, a list size, and a *span* value to run.

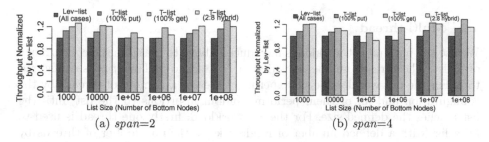

(a) *span*=2                    (b) *span*=4

**Fig. 4.** Normalized performance with different sized lists. For 100% put, the list is inserted with random keys from blank to the size. For 100% get, the list is first constructed by 100% put to the size, and then search 1 million random keys. For 20% put 80% get, every operation is determined by this ratio and 5 times the size operations are processed.

Fig. 4a and b give the results of all the experiments normalized by Lev-list grouped by the list size, with span configured to 2 and 4 respectively. We can see that when $span = 2$, T-list has better performance in all cases. When $span$ is configured to 4, T-list also performs better except when the list size is $10^5$ and $10^6$. As T-list builds index stations on the search phase when inserting a node and generates faster paths for later operations, its advantage may not show up when the list size is small under the put workload. When the list size increases, T-list can build a stable index structure and a single insert operation benefits well from it. Lev-list uses probability mechanism to build index nodes that can have varied list height in a same experiment. Figure 5 demonstrates the height variances that are calculated from the put workload experiments. Although Lev-list has the expected height for a given list size, it intends to generates a more higher structure than the expected value, which makes the search operations traverses more paths to the bottom. This can be reflected from the result of the get workload, in which T-list always performs better than Lev-list in any cases no matter the $span$ value. As the get workload works on a static list, the experiment results can reflect that T-list generates a more perfect and efficient index structures.

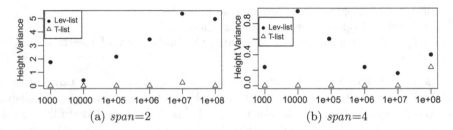

(a) $span=2$                    (b) $span=4$

**Fig. 5.** Height variance of constructing different sized lists. The result comes from the 100% put workload. Every experiment is repeated five times and the heights are recorded for computing the variance.

### 4.2  Multi-thread

We use the put and get workloads introduced above to evaluate the concurrency of T-list. The threads number is varied in 1, 2, 4 and 8. The $span$ is configured to 2. For the put workload, each experiment creates a number of threads by the configuration and all of them perform random insertions to the list until the list reaches the defined size. For the get workload, firstly one thread is used to fill a list with a defined number of random keys, then a number of threads by the configuration are created to do random searches on the list until totally 10 million requests are processed.

Figure 6a and b show the results of the put and get workloads with different threads running on varied sized lists. The figures show that, while multi-threads is more efficient for the large sized list, it degrades the performance when the list size is small. This is comprehensible since there are overheads of the threads management work, which emerge to be significantly when the overheads on normal operations are small.

Specifically for the put workload, a lock is shared in all threads for adding a station on a same path. In small sized list the threads are more likely to contend for locks because only few paths can be operated at the same time. With the list size increasing, the overheads for contending locks are distributed as the search route becomes long. As search operations do not need to acquire locks, theoretically they do not suffer the contention overheads that are significant in the small list. However, the scalability of multi-threads for the get workload also is achieved when the size increases. This can be resulted from the high proportion of scheduling overheads in concurrently accessing small portion of data.

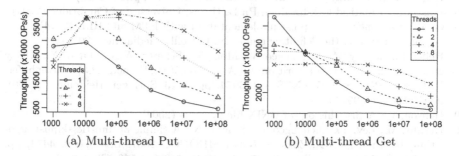

(a) Multi-thread Put                          (b) Multi-thread Get

**Fig. 6.** Threads scalability in different sized lists, the span configured to 2. The threads number are varied from 1 to 8. For the put workload, different number of threads are created and they concurrently insert random keys to the list until it reaches the size. For the get workload, a list is first created to the determined size by one thread with random keys, and then different number of threads are created to do concurrent search operations in this list (totally a million random keys are processed).

## 5   Conclusion

In this paper we introduce and implement a skip list construction algorithm, called T-list, that employs a special search procedure to build indexes according to the traversing steps on the search progress. Building-on-search makes the index construction work distributed on the search phases so as the heavy operations on the new nodes are relieved. Besides, T-list maintains loose constraint rules to make the index structure self-adjustable according to the workload patterns for insert-intensive workloads. On the other hand, concurrent operations can benefit from T-list as each update to the structure only needs to lock two nodes on a single path. The evaluations on the prototype show that T-list achieves better performance than the skip list used in LevelDB. For multi-core environments it also performs well in the scalability with the increasing number of threads.

Nevertheless, more potential properties can be exploited from T-list. As the real-world workloads are varied, a more intelligent algorithm that can fit varied environments is worthwhile to be studied. We plan to improve the algorithm in the future by leveraging its adjustable characteristic to make it aware of and intelligent to the complex and varied use cases.

# References

1. Chang, F., et al.: Bigtable: a distributed storage system for structured data. ACM Trans. Comput. Syst. (TOCS) **26**(2), 4 (2008)
2. Clouser, T., Nesterenko, M., Scheideler, C.: Tiara: a self-stabilizing deterministic skip list. In: Kulkarni, S., Schiper, A. (eds.) SSS 2008. LNCS, vol. 5340, pp. 124–140. Springer, Heidelberg (2008). doi:10.1007/978-3-540-89335-6_12
3. Crain, T., Gramoli, V., Raynal, M.: No hot spot non-blocking skip list. In: IEEE 33rd International Conference on Distributed Computing Systems (ICDCS), pp. 196–205. IEEE (2013)
4. Dean, J., Ghemawat, S.: LevelDB. In: Retrieved, vol. 1, p. 12 (2012)
5. Fraser, K.: Practical lock-freedom. Ph.D. thesis. University of Cambridge (2004)
6. Gao, F.: A concurrent skip list implementation with RTM and HLE (2014)
7. George, L.: HBase: the definitive guide. In: O'Reilly Media, Inc. (2011)
8. Heller, S., Herlihy, M., Luchangco, V., Moir, M., Scherer, W.N., Shavit, N.: A lazy concurrent list-based set algorithm. In: Anderson, J.H., Prencipe, G., Wattenhofer, R. (eds.) OPODIS 2005. LNCS, vol. 3974, pp. 3–16. Springer, Heidelberg (2006). doi:10.1007/11795490_3
9. Henson, V.: A Brief history of UNIX file systems (2004)
10. Herlihy, M., Lev, Y., Luchangco, V., Shavit, N.: A simple optimistic skiplist algorithm. In: Prencipe, G., Zaks, S. (eds.) SIROCCO 2007. LNCS, vol. 4474, pp. 124–138. Springer, Heidelberg (2007). doi:10.1007/978-3-540-72951-8_11
11. Lakshman, A., Malik, P.: Cassandra: a decentralized structured storage system. ACM SIGOPS Operating Syst. Rev. **44**(2), 35–40 (2010)
12. MemSQL. MemSQL Documentation. http://docs.memsql.com/4.1/concepts/indexes/
13. Munro, J.I., Papadakis, T., Sedgewick, R.: Deterministic skip lists. In: Proceedings of the Third Annual ACM-SIAM Symposium on Discrete algorithms. Society for Industrial and Applied Mathematics, pp. 367–375 (1992)
14. Pugh, W.: Concurrent maintenance of skip lists (1990)
15. Pugh, W.: Skip lists: a probabilistic alternative to balanced trees. Commun. ACM **33**(6), 668–676 (1990)
16. Sémon, P., et al.: Lazy skip-lists: an algorithm for fast hybridization-expansion quantum Monte Carlo. Phys. Rev. B **90**(7), 075149 (2014)
17. Shamgunov, N.: The MemSQL in-memory database system. In: IMDM@ VLDB (2014)
18. Singh, R., Chakraborty, S., Karmakar, S.: Concurrent deterministic 1–2 skip list in distributed message passing systems. Int. J. Parallel Emergent Distrib. Syst. **30**(2), 135–174 (2015)
19. Timnat, S., Braginsky, A., Kogan, A., Petrank, E.: Wait-free linked-lists. In: Baldoni, R., Flocchini, P., Binoy, R. (eds.) OPODIS 2012. LNCS, vol. 7702, pp. 330–344. Springer, Heidelberg (2012). doi:10.1007/978-3-642-35476-2_23

# Author Index

Printed in the United States
By Bookmasters